WHISPERS
IN THE STILLNESS

Mindfulness and Spiritual Awakening

MARTINA LEHANE SHEEHAN

VERITA

Published 2014 by
Veritas Publications
7–8 Lower Abbey Street
Dublin 1
Ireland
publications@veritas.ie
www.veritas.ie

ISBN 978 1 84730 555 8

10 9 8 7 6 5 4 3 2

The opening epigraph is Paul Murray's 'The World Within You',
The Absent Fountain (Dublin: Dedalus Press, 1991), p. 12.

A catalogue record for this book is available from the British Library.

Designed by Dara O'Connor, Veritas
Printed in Ireland by W&G Baird Ltd, Antrim

*Veritas books are printed on paper made from the wood pulp of managed forests.
For every tree felled, at least one tree is planted, thereby renewing natural resources.*

There is a world within you
no one has ever seen,
a voice no one has ever heard,
not even you.
As yet unknown
you are your own seer,
your own interpreter.
And so, with eyes and ears
grown sharp, for voice or sign,
listen well –
not to these words
but to that inward voice,
that impulse beating in your heart
like a far wave.
Turn to that source, and you
will find
what no one has ever found,
a ground within you
no one has ever seen,
a world beyond the limits
of your dream's horizon.

Paul Murray, 'The World Within You'

ACKNOWLEDGEMENTS

Whispers in the Stillness was written sitting by the window in the precious hours of early mornings, so I owe gratitude to the dawn chorus, a lighted candle and numerous cups of coffee. While I wrote in solitude, every word that poured onto the page was prompted and inspired in some way by the amazing people who grace my path each day: friends, family, colleagues and chance encounters. You are all in here, so thank you.

Thanks to all at Veritas Publications who continue to believe in my writing; to Julie, my editor, for your non-intrusive suggestions.

Finally, thanks to Pat, whom this book is dedicated to; through your unassuming presence you teach more about stillness and mindfulness than any book could aspire to.

CONTENTS

Introduction

This book has come about mainly as a response to requests from readers of my previous book, *Seeing Anew: Awakening to Life's Lessons.* Many people who read it remarked how it introduced an implicit integration of mindfulness with spirituality, and so suggested the possibility of another book which would develop that relationship further. Because mindfulness has become such a popular concept these days, with no shortage of books already written on the subject, I wasn't so sure at first. However, on deeper exploration it became clear that many, including myself, are searching for a way to integrate mindfulness with their spirituality and their faith. My work in accompanying and listening to others on retreats, as well as in counselling, psychotherapy and spiritual direction, has brought me into contact with numerous people who are searching for a deeper rhythmic listening, where they are more disposed to hear not just their own voice, but to intuit the Divine *whispers in the stillness.*

The recent upsurge of interest in mindfulness comes primarily from its scientifically measured benefits for mental health and well-being. Mindfulness is both a practice and a way of life which teaches us to become more fully aware, awake and attentive to the present moment. It is an embracing and a compassionate turning towards both inner and outer experiences, whether those experiences are pleasant or painful.

While there is increased interest in mindfulness at present, especially in its association with Buddhist teaching, its concepts are not new, nor are they exclusive to Buddhism. Indeed, the practice of mindfulness has echoes in both eastern and western traditions, and its concepts have strong parallels with Christian contemplation. These parallels will be considered in this book, along with an exploration of how mindfulness and spirituality can be pathways to healing. These themes will be developed, not in an abstract or conceptual way, but through real-life stories and reflections, as well as insights from the wisdom of scripture, transpersonal psychology and the great spiritual writers. This will be underpinned by short mindfulness meditations.

The mind–body–spirit approach in this book aims to amalgamate the practice of mindfulness with psychological and spiritual awareness. It guides us towards becoming more attentive to the present moment, more attentive to the psychological patterns and blocks that prevent us from being present; most importantly, it demonstrates how we might surrender those blocks to a higher power. This emphasis on surrender is often a missing dimension in some popularised mindfulness practices, but when integrated can be a pathway for transformation. The image of clouds in the mind is often used in mindfulness – perhaps it could be said that mindfulness brings awareness of those clouds, psychology helps to roll them back, while spirituality invokes the sun. This book invites you to bask in the sun!

How To Use This Book

You may wish to dip in and out of the chapters or read them through chronologically. However you choose to read it, the primary aim of this book is to encourage you to spend time creating space to let the wellsprings of awareness and healing rise within you. Therefore, it would be helpful to keep a journal at hand whereby you could jot down what may arise unexpectedly and where you could ask yourself some questions and wait, allowing the answers to unfold in their own time. This can be aided through engaging in the reflective exercises at the end of each chapter. These are designed to help you dig a little deeper into the themes presented in the stories so that you can integrate and discern how they might be a catalyst for your own story and what of their themes may be true for you. This will require a small expenditure of effort on your part but will reward you immeasurably by uncovering and transforming the roots of the many autopilot habits, patterns and reactions that occupy our days. Such digging will guide you towards a more intentional rhythmic daily mindfulness, without which we remain unaware of the treasures waiting to be discovered in each moment. The exercises lead you firstly into a moment of mindfulness, then to a discernment of the deeper patterns you carry in your life and in your heart, and finally towards a resting into the source of healing. You are then invited into a closing blessing, whereby your reflection and awareness can become a source of healing for others. While this section appears as four numbered steps, this is merely for clarity in reading; they are more movements than a rigid sequence, since our spiritual journey is very much a non-linear process.

My own background, study and training in psychology and spirituality may play a part in the explorations in this book, however, much of the wisdom and inspiration herein comes from day-to-day life – both my own and that of others. While the stories are often deeply personal, you will notice they are also your stories because our issues tend to be universal and, when reflected upon, seem no longer as random happenings, but reveal themselves as opportunities for us to become more awake and aware. Some of the stories are funny, some are poignant; some of the described events take place in shops, cafes and trains, because any person, place or thing can provide us with an 'epiphany moment' – a moment of awareness through which our lives can be changed irrevocably.

This book can act as a home-based retreat. You do not need to travel to anywhere extraordinary to begin to inhale and savour the wonder of the present moment; you can create a little hermitage in your own home and in your own heart. Maybe light a candle or put your feet up with a cup of coffee. Of course, you will not be the only beneficiary of this reflective time; when we take time out, others become transformed by our renewed presence – perhaps they too will hear their own whispers in the stillness.

CHAPTER 1

Whispers at Dawn:
Lessons from the Silence

I jumped out of bed. My watch showed it was a quarter to nine. Breakfast in the monastery was at nine and I did not want to be late on my first morning. I stumbled down to the dining room, curtains still drawn in both the room and my mind. I waited for a while; still not a sound throughout the monastery. I drew back the curtains and noticed it was still dark outside, hardly a glimmer of the dawn emerging. I looked at my watch again and realised it was not a quarter to nine – it was a quarter to six! So there I was, alone in the dining room where breakfast would not be served for another three hours. I had made up my mind to go back to bed but the gently swaying trees still lit up by the waning moon seemed to suggest otherwise. The words of a poem that I once read came back to me:

The breeze at dawn
has secrets to tell you.

Don't go back to sleep.

You must ask
for what you really want.

Don't go back to sleep.

People are going back and forth
across the doorsill
where the two worlds touch.

The door is round and open.

Don't go back to sleep.[1]

I felt drawn to the window and sat there for what must have been hours, just looking out over a sleeping city. I do not usually like the dark, but there was a strange comfort in this pre-dawn darkness, it seemed to be filled with possibility, as if there was a door round and open in my consciousness. All thoughts of breakfast faded; thoughts of going back to bed no longer pressed. I was like the seed waiting silently in the dark soil for some tiny shoot of new life. Eventually, the first glimmer of the dawn appeared and a chink of light awakened within me a new sense of wonder. In Celtic tradition, dawn and dusk are often referred to as 'thin places'. At dawn the unconscious and the conscious world embrace, the visible and invisible, the internal and external, the sleeping and waking all touch each other in this veiled numinous space. This subtle boundary, known as a threshold or an 'in-between' place, is considered a time of inspiration where the two worlds touch. The breezes at dawn could whisper their secrets now because I was wide awake. I became aware that an unfamiliar peace was emanating from the very place I feared – the empty alone place within, the space I saw as a type of black hole that could swallow me up. I usually try to fill that hole with projects, events or work, but now that I was not filling it – was sitting here alone – the blackness

1 'The Breeze at Dawn', *The Essential Rumi*, Coleman Barks, trans. (San Francisco: HarperSanFrancisco, 2004), p. 16.

was not black anymore; it was strangely comforting, serene, sacred even. I began to feel that perhaps I was not alone after all, but surrounded by those going 'back and forth across the doorsill'.

I didn't know why I had wanted to come here, to this lonely place. It was just something I needed to do. It felt like a response to the scriptural invitation to 'come away to a quiet place and rest for a while' (Mk 6:31). Well-meaning friends said, 'Are you mad? You're going to miss a great weekend.' It was the October bank holiday – an especially active time in Cork when the annual jazz festival takes place. Each year a group of us would meet up and go from pub to pub to hear all the different bands. I loved the atmosphere, the buzz. As usual, there were a few concerts I had been really looking forward to. So it was difficult to face this fork in the road and choose an alternative route – one that would mean missing out and letting my friends down. Nevertheless, something inside beckoned me towards this retreat, which was entitled Desert Space.

As the sun rose, a single bird competed with the sounds of an awakening city preparing for the festival. The early morning bustle began. I thought about the drivers of the vans passing in the distance on the road below, each going about their early morning rituals, delivering bread, milk and other provisions; each part of the great web of life. I still felt part of that web, even way up here in this secluded monastery. I had a strange feeling of being apart, yet part of the activity of the city. I did not feel disconnected in this solitude; in fact, I felt more connected than I often felt in a crowded room. This led me to wonder if it is by embracing the frequently avoided but essential aloneness that we discover our greatest resources, freeing ourselves from the slavish expectations of hoping that someone or something will fill our aloneness. Is it when we stop expecting others to rescue us that we can bring more of ourselves into life? Is it when we give our eyes a rest from the sensory overload of bright lights that we find glimmers of the soft light within? Maybe it is only then that we can find wholeness instead of connecting with only half of ourselves and waiting for life to send us our 'other half'. That seemed to be the first 'whisper at dawn', and many more were to follow in the coming days during this retreat.

Just Sit and Listen

During the first couple of days I was filled with a sense of wonder, helped by the lovely sunrises and birdsong each morning. I thought every day would be like this but, alas, there were to be grey days. I was scheduled to meet with a spiritual director for a short period each day. By day three, although I was still enjoying the early morning sunrises, my feet and heart felt heavy. All consolation was gone. The initial joy and wonder I had felt had suddenly dried up and I wanted to run away. I started to read the books I had packed for my journey just to fill the time rather than for inspiration. Much to my horror, on this third day the director suggested I put away all books and embrace a spirit of mindfulness through silence and inactivity. 'Absurd,' I decided as he further insisted I 'take nothing for the journey today, not even those books'. For the next couple of days the only interlude would be the short check-in with the director, who happened to be a very quiet man.

I looked miserably at the rain outside, at my empty bookshelves. 'They're out to get me,' I decided as I paced the floor. What was I to do? 'Just sit and listen,' the director had suggested. Listen to what? To the jazz festival in the distance and my thoughts telling me how crazy I was not to have gone? To the ticking clock or the annoying dripping sound from a drainpipe outside my window? Even the idea of climbing the pipe to fix it now seemed more attractive than sitting with this nothingness, which the director had referred to as 'mindfulness'. I once saw a quotation which read 'deep within your soul there is a knowing place, a sanctuary'.[2] This felt much more like a prison than a sanctuary. 'Just sit and listen,' I heard the director say again in my head. So I sat – on the chair, on the floor, on the bed – and tried to listen. I sat crossed-legged, I sat with palms faced upwards, then downwards, looking at my watch (which I was convinced had stopped). At dinnertime I sat in silence with the others. How I longed to talk about anything – the weather, even the economy. But I couldn't even catch their eye. As we put away our plates, I decided, with new enthusiasm, I would do the washing up. At least it would pass some time, I thought. Then I saw a notice asking us to leave the dishes on the trolley – even washing up wasn't allowed! I started thinking of how badly I wanted chocolate, and so went to the biscuit tin, where there were only plain, wrinkled digestives. I went to the coffee jar – it was decaf!

The day passed slowly. I tried a few more contorted praying positions, hoping for some sudden epiphany, a flash of light – but nothing. I slept badly that night, waking at intervals, heart hammering. I dreamt that the steering wheel of my car was missing. With increasing paranoia, I thought about how 'they' had taken everything from me: my books, chocolate, coffee, and now my steering wheel! I so wanted to take back control of my life.

---

2 Macrina Wiederkehr, 'The Song of the Seed', *The Monastic Way of Tending the Soul* (San Francisco: HarperSanFrancisco, 1995), p. 113.

Losing Grip

The next morning at breakfast, the only thing audible was an awful slurping sound from across the table, coming from a toothless woman who seemed to be drinking her cornflakes. I wondered if 'they' had taken her teeth. I tried to turn it to a positive by expressing gratitude that I, at least, still had my teeth. 'They have taken everything else, but no one,' I insisted, 'no one will ever take my teeth!' Of course, that night I dreamt of losing my teeth. The director told me the dream was related to fear of losing control and suggested I think a little more about what it could mean. He smiled at me, displaying his own perfect rows.

Outside the rain poured down. I went back to the same window where I'd had the beautiful dawn experience the first couple of mornings. Thoughts of yesterday and tomorrow filled my mind. Anything but today! Anything but my chattering mind, the sound of the rain, the longing for real coffee, the irritating sound of someone slurping or snoring! As if on cue, a dog barked in the distance. I wondered who had arranged for him to do so just as I was starting my meditation. I began to hold mental conversations with the dog but he refused to *sit and listen*, he just seemed to bark all the louder. I was fighting a losing battle. Soon I would have my check-in with the director, which seemed like a waste of time. I didn't see the point in repeatedly meeting a man who, each time I visited, only smiled gingerly and told me to 'sit and listen'. I wished he would advise me, tell me what to do. Maybe I should check his credentials; maybe he wasn't trained properly. Maybe I should just leave today.

There followed another disturbed night, this time with dreams of being chased by the barking dog, and he, unfortunately, had no shortage of teeth. I began to grumble.

Didn't Jesus have angels watching out for him in the desert? Who was watching out for me? I looked around for an angel – all I saw smiling back was my toothless fellow retreatant.

Giving Up the Fight

With no energy left to fight, I found myself unable to do anything except rest. I gradually surrendered the maybes and the fighting mind. I resisted nothing. And somehow, after a while, I no longer even heard the dog barking, the dripping pipe, or the slurping, or felt the coffee craving, or fought the rain. I was just being in the present moment. Present to the breath, neither wishing for things to be like yesterday nor escaping into tomorrow. By ceasing to escape from the present moment, by no longer wishing for a different set of circumstances, I discovered a new type of silence, a richer one, amidst the orchestra of the daily sounds. I could even see beauty in the rain hitting the window pane. A peace seemed to descend and settle in my heart like morning dew, gradually dispelling the restless dark night of the soul. It was a soft, shy kind of peace – a gentle dawn whisper in the stillness, one that could be very easily missed unless one was willing to simply sit and listen.

Lessons From the 'Desert'

The 'desert' retreat was at times a place of emptiness – a place where I met some of my own demons, where the silence was teaching me to let go of the control over my life. Most of all it showed me the value of existing in the present moment. The restlessness I experienced taught me something about mindfulness: how much of the suffering of our lives comes from resistance, either through wanting what we do not have or not wanting what we do have. Mindfulness is about finding stillness amidst noise, peace within turbulence and a shelter within a storm. I had to learn to cultivate the same stillness and mindfulness in the midst of the daily cacophony as I had in tranquil settings. My inner silence had to become big enough and broad enough to recognise that birdsong and breezes are not the only teachers of mindfulness.

As I made my way back from the retreat to my everyday life, I wasn't so much on autopilot and was less entangled in the trance of routine habits and reactions. I was more aware and awake. I looked at the shopkeeper as she handed me my change rather than reading the headlines of the newspaper. I didn't complain about traffic; I used the waiting time at the red lights to pause and breathe. The mundane was charged with beauty, all because I had taken a few days to reduce stimulation in order to listen to the silence.

Though this desert experience is now a far distant memory, I continue to rise each morning, twenty years on, and take some time to just sit and listen.

Whispers at Dawn

You too can begin a journey of listening to your own *whispers at dawn*. Choose a seat, a corner of a room or a quiet place that will become your sacred space; it will be your own retreat, so give time to creating it. You could include in this space things that are conducive to reflection, things that are meaningful to you. Maybe light a candle and dedicate this sacred place and journey to your transformation:

> May morning be astir with the harvest of night;
> Your mind quickening to the eros of a new question,
> Your eyes seduced by some unintended glimpse
> That cut right through the surface to a source.

May this be a morning of innocent beginning,
When the gift within you slips clear
Of the sticky web of the personal
With its hurt and its hauntings,
And fixed fortress corners,

A Morning when you become a pure vessel
For what wants to ascend from silence ...[3]

A Moment for Mindfulness

1. Take a moment of silence, become aware of your breathing in this present moment. Be aware of what you are doing – perhaps avoiding the silence, planning things in your head – just acknowledge this. Notice how you try to escape, perhaps by running through stories in your head. Again, do not judge these thoughts just be aware of them. Now, bring your awareness of these patterns of 'escape' into a more bodily awareness. Allow a deeper layer to unfold: When did you first learn to escape in your life? How did this serve you then? How does it serve you now?

2. In order to let further insights emerge, write in your journal about any difficulties you might have with silence. What do you fear you might find in the silence? What do you think you might gain?

3. Bring whatever has arisen into a silent prayer, surrendering it to the God of your awareness.

---

3 John O'Donohue, *Benedictus: A Book of Blessings* (London: Transworld, 2007), p. 35.

4. A suggested closing blessing:

May I, and all people, this day find freedom from unrest.
May we be awake and aware.

CHAPTER 2

The Desert Within:
A Heart of Mindfulness

The desert appears frequently in scripture as a place for reflection, listening and discernment and as a place of encounter. In the Old Testament we meet the Israelites wandering in the desert for forty years. The prophet Hosea was told by God that Israel would be led to the desert, where God would speak: 'That is why I am going to lure her and lead her out into the wilderness and speak to her heart' (Hos 2:14). In the New Testament John the Baptist went out into the desert, where he wore camel clothing and ate locusts and wild honey. Jesus, at the beginning of his ministry, went into the desert – to a dry, arid, stony, silent place filled with obstacles and danger. Likewise, nearly two thousand years ago, the early desert fathers and mothers, hermits, ascetics and monks lived a simple desert spirituality of solitude in small communities.

From Trance to Transformation
There seems to be a new call today. More and more people are taking soul journeys, becoming drawn to times of silence, rituals and pilgrimages. Many of us are going on retreats, mindfulness and meditation courses, creating communities of new monasticism, going to hermitages and walking the Camino. This soul cry seems to be emerging from a collective

dark night of the soul, almost like a spiritual epidemic. Amidst a culture obsessed with speed and technological advancement, people are awakening from the trance of social hypnotism. Perhaps the cultural milieu is evolving, and with it is coming a new call to live more radically, to strip back the artificiality of our lives.

Mindfulness is one of the things helping us to become more awake, bringing a spirit of attentiveness, compassion and non-judgement to our lives. It shows us how we can exercise more choice in our responses and reactions to everyday events, while bringing awareness to the mental states and patterns that limit us. Through it we learn to accept both what we label as pleasurable or painful with less preference and therefore with less resistance, thus restoring our inner balance. Becoming aware and awake helps us live with more peace and less attachment. This lessening in attachment does not lead to less involvement but to more spaciousness and freedom; through it we create space for noticing, enquiring and listening. Mindfulness teaches us that whenever we become embroiled in obsessive thinking, we can gently bring the mind back to the present moment. We do so by attending to the breath and by simply observing those times when the mind wanders off. This helps to identify whatever has captured the mind, for example by naming whether it is 'fear', 'control' or 'worry'. The very act of naming brings us back and endorses the fact that while we may *have* worry, we are *not* worry, while we may *have* fear, we are *not* fear. The natural self – free of such states and present to the moment – can then float to the surface of our awareness, bringing a renewed wonder, awe and freshness into our daily lives. This simple practice, when done throughout the day, creates a new attentiveness.

A Place of Encounter

While a lot of contemporary mindfulness literature is underpinned by a Buddhist philosophy, there is much written on Christian mindfulness which has not been brought into the public domain. A lot of contemplatives, such as Teresa of Ávila, John of the Cross, Catherine of Siena and Thomas Merton, have written extensively on the concept of having an inner desert, a place of stillness and silence. Saint Isaac the Syrian advises us to 'love silence above all things, because it brings you near to the fruit that the tongue cannot express'.[4] From out of this silence something is born that leads to silence itself. In returning to this inner silence and developing what is sometimes call 'watchfulness', we observe the many mental states that we can get caught up in. In doing so, we can thwart the exhausting, continuous circular thinking. The 'something born' is ultimately the awareness of the Divine living at the core of our being: 'the deeper I descend into myself, the more I find God at the heart of my being.'[5] Many writers and mystics describe this inner stillness as leading to a dwelling place of divine mystery: 'to find love I must enter into the Sanctuary where it is hidden, which is the mystery of God.'[6] This search for the 'mystery of God' awakens in many when they begin to explore a practice of mindfulness; they begin to discover that we have an innate longing for the Divine. (This notion is further developed in the section on Contemplative Prayer in chapter eight.)

---

4 St Isaac the Syrian, 'On Silence', *The Ascetical Homilies of Isaac the Syrian* (Boston: Holy Transfiguration Monastery, 1984), p. 310.

5 Pierre Teilhard de Chardin, *Writings* (Maryknoll, NY: Orbis Books, 1999), p. 50.

6 Thomas Merton, *New Seeds of Contemplation* (New York: New Directions, 2007), p. 61.

Of course people mean different things when they speak of 'mindfulness'. For some, it is a living in the moment, a consciousness; while for many it is a tool for mental health and well-being. However one identifies it, there is a way of being mindful where one cultivates being present *to* the moment and to the 'presence' *in* the moment. This is where mindfulness and spirituality can converge. When we return to the present moment, noticing the passing of thoughts, mental activity and all else that is transient, we discover an inner spaciousness and emptiness. When we open and surrender that empty space, we experience this emptiness as fullness.

Recall the image of the parting clouds and the sun; in marrying mindfulness and spirituality, it is as if the clouds (of mental activity) part, revealing a new stillness where we become aware that we are all suffused in some warming, nurturing presence which we call 'God'.

An Unshakable Stillness

We can find strength in stillness. In Zen meditation, this stillness is sometimes captured by the image of a mountain which remains steadfast even amidst the swirling storms. Likewise, in scripture this stillness and unshakability is compared to Mount Zion: 'Those who trust in Yahweh are like Mount Zion, unshakable, standing for ever. Jerusalem! Encircled by mountains, as Yahweh encircled his people' (Ps 125:1-2).

However, you do not have to climb a distant mountain to find stillness; you carry that mountain within. Anchored on this unshakable mountain, you do not have to react to every passing storm, you can remain peaceful, grounded, serene no matter how busy your external life becomes. When you find your home in stillness, you can be at home anywhere. In the words of Kafka:

It isn't necessary that you leave home. Sit at your desk and listen. Don't even listen, just wait. Don't wait, be still and alone. The whole world will offer itself to you to be unmasked, it can do no other, it will writhe before you in ecstasy.[7]

Mindful Mornings

I used to wake to the sound of the radio coming on, until one morning I woke to the news headlines informing me of a stabbing the night before. All day I had an edgy, jumpy feeling. So, just as we eat a healthy breakfast to sustain us throughout the day, we also need to start the day with healthy images in the mind. We need to be mindful of what we let into our subconscious first thing in the morning. We can shape the day by sowing seeds of gratitude and beauty instead of seeds of violence and negativity: 'It is the soft light just before the dawn in which our shy and elusive inner self gazes through the lattice, communicating to us the first silent syllables of the unspeakable secret.'[8] This 'soft light' illuminates our inner world, calling us to hear those faint little whispers that are often trampled on by the day's events. Dawn is a time when this soft light awakens a sleeping world to a new beginning, when we breathe anew all that this day has to offer. Those hours early in the morning can be a valuable pearl, a precious time when we can connect with our shy and elusive inner self.

---

7   Franz Kafka, *The Zürau Aphorisms*, Roberto Calasso, ed., Michael Hoffman and Geoffrey Brok, trans. (New York: Schocken, 2006), p. 108.
8   James Finley, *Merton's Palace of Nowhere* (Notre Dame, IN: Ave Maria Press, 1978), p. 81.

Waking Up

The early morning stillness is a time when the mystery of life can be revealed to us, like Mary at the tomb on the first Easter Sunday morning where she encountered the Risen Christ. The morning quiet offers the opportunity to listen and intuit things that become inaccessible when daytime activities take over our minds. Some Jewish literature sees the body and soul as 'married' to one another, suggesting that they go their separate ways while we are asleep. It suggests that, during this time, the soul can travel beyond time and space to pick up information from deeply buried material in the unconscious and collective unconscious. The body and soul unite again upon waking: 'a new day is like a wedding, with your blanket as the *chupah* or marriage canopy. So take a moment each morning to celebrate the joy of this reunion, and sing *Modeh Ani*, "I give thanks".'[9] If we start each new day as if it was a wedding or a banquet, we would enter into it with a spirit of celebration, sacramentality and awe. When we awake with an intentional attentiveness, the day's activities tend to unfold and flow from one's being rather than through mindless reactionary habits. In this way, we are less tangled in the transitory or the negative moods that can hold us captive. Instead, we become more mindful of the present moment and the inner meaning and wisdom of each experience.

A Clear Eye

'If your eye is clear, then your whole body will be filled with light' (Mt 6:22). Morning is a good time to cultivate

---

9 Tamar Frankiel and Judy Greenfield, *Minding the Temple of the Soul: Balancing Body, Mind and Spirit Through Traditional Jewish Prayer Movement and Meditation* (Woodstock, VT: Jewish Lights Publishing, 1997), p. 26.

the 'clear eye', which includes becoming aware of autopilot reactions and those things which prevent us from being aware and seeing things clearly. There is much each day that can cause the eye to cloud over, precluding any real sense of wonder or present-moment aliveness.

Mindfulness helps us become aware of the subtle belief systems and filters through which we meet the events and circumstances of each day. We wake up from mindless trances when we realise that it is usually our own conditioned beliefs that limit us, and not something 'out there'. A significant measure of freedom arises when you discover that some of the pain or misery in your life is compounded by the stories you tell yourself: 'you wrap yourself in thoughts the way a spider wraps flies in gossamer, you are both the spider and the fly, entangling yourself in your own web.'[10]

There's Always Something

I once knew a woman people referred to as Mrs Misery. They tended to cross the road when they saw her coming – she always had a bad story to tell, and usually finished it off by saying 'Sure, there's always something'. This woman was miserable because she reaffirmed negativity through the stories she repeatedly told herself and others. When we complain that 'there's always something' or 'poor me', we add what mindfulness calls 'secondary suffering' to our primary suffering. We increase our pain when we believe that we are the only ones with this misfortune; we add pain when we judge something as being 'terrible' or 'awful'. A moment of mindfulness interrupts these running commentaries so that we can get in touch with our real pain. This creates space

10 Deepak Chopra, *Power, Freedom and Grace: Living From the Source of Lasting Happiness* (San Rafael, CA: Amber-Allen Publishing Inc., 2006), p. 164.

for the light of healing to get in. Even during a night of insomnia, by continually telling yourself 'this is terrible, I have to be up early tomorrow', you are adding secondary anxiety and are likely to toss and turn even more. All of us encounter pain – the inevitable losses, disappointments and limitations of life – but the mind can add an extra layer of stress and, in doing so, close us off and close us in, preventing the light of awareness from reaching us. We can even get comfortable in this closed and suffocating existence. Seamus Heaney, in his poem 'The Skylight', identifies something of this preference for the 'low and closed':

> You were the one for skylights. I opposed
> Cutting into the seasoned tongue-and-groove
> Of pitch pine. I liked it low and closed,
> Its claustrophobic, nest-up-in-the-roof
> Effect. I liked the snuff-dry feeling,
> The perfect, trunk-lid fit of the old ceiling.
> Under there, it was all hutch and hatch.
> The blue slates kept the heat like midnight thatch.
> But when the slates came off, extravagant
> Sky entered and held surprise wide open.
> For days I felt like an inhabitant
> Of that house where the man sick of the palsy
> Was lowered through the roof, had his sins forgiven,
> Was healed, took up his bed and walked away.[11]

Here, Heaney describes his own resistance to letting go of the place of suffocation, the 'snuff-dry feeling'. His fear of the slates being removed, the sky entering and his being

---

11 Seamus Heaney, 'The Skylight', *Seeing Things* (London: Faber and Faber, 1991), p. 37.

'wide open' speaks to all of us. His poem echoes the scripture account of the man being lowered on a stretcher through an opening in the roof: 'but as they could find no way of getting him through the crowd, they went up on top of the house and lowered him and his stretcher down through the tiles into the middle of the gathering, in front of Jesus' (Mk 2:4). We too can stay 'low and closed' through a type of armouring when we tighten our hearts and our muscles, what can be described medically as neuromuscular contraction. We can defend against feelings of vulnerability by employing obsessive mental activity, as well as shallow breathing, both of which keep us sensitised and numb, keeping in 'the heat like midnight thatch'. When we open ourselves up to the reality of these compensatory defences, we create space for the light to get in. Through a few moments of mindful awareness, we notice how this limited mental chatter can become like a 'claustrophobic nest-up-in-the-roof'. When we detach from this chatter and allow a few slates to come off, the 'extravagant sky' can enter. The limitless supply of Divine providence can become visible through this new opening.

A Moment for Mindfulness

1. Become aware of the present moment and the rise and fall of your breath. Acknowledge the busy mind (up in the roof). Become aware of the stories and running commentaries in your head. Don't judge them; just name and notice. Now return to the breath. Become aware of your body and notice how some of those stories and belief systems can affect you, perhaps tightening and contracting your muscles.

2. Write about those ways you sometimes add secondary suffering to your pain. What mental drama does your mind add? Could it be some version of 'nothing good happens to me, I always miss the boat' or 'there's always something'? Write down, without judgement, these things you habitually tell yourself.

3. Surrender those empty spaces that lie between thoughts to the 'extravagant light'.

4. A suggested closing blessing:

> *May I, and each of us, discover the extravagant light,*
> *in which we all breathe, live, move and have our being.*

CHAPTER 3

In Search of Bliss:
The Marriage of Mindfulness
and Spirituality

The view was breathtaking. Pat and I had just climbed a mountain and could see for miles out over the Atlantic Ocean. We stood in silence for a few minutes trying to take it in. The sun glistened across the water, the mountains in the distance still peaked with snow, but it was hot and balmy here in Spain. A seamless beauty enveloped us. Apart from the distant sound of the ocean and the faint sound of crickets, all was quiet. I was a mere speck, standing before the enormity of the mountains and the vastness of the ocean. Feeling so small and insignificant in the face of this awesome mystery was unnerving; to be without words was disconcerting, so much so that I began to babble, 'Look at this beautiful scene … the tranquility and peace … look at the snow on the mountains…' Receiving no reply, I continued, 'Listen to the sound of the crickets, the swelling of the ocean …' Eventually Pat replied softly, 'Yes, but it would be lovely if there was enough silence to actually *hear* the ocean.' I still didn't get the hint and continued, 'Wouldn't it be lovely if we could afford an apartment here? We could escape the Irish winters. Or wouldn't it be lovely to retire here …' Pat interrupted, less softly this time, 'Could you not just be in the present moment and take it in?' Embarrassed, I realised that instead of receiving and savouring this momentary gift, I was trying to possess it, to make it permanent, filling the silence with unnecessary words. It was as if the spaciousness and silence was so threatening to my busy mind, it began to objectify, control and possess. When we get caught up in possessing and craving, we slide into a mirage that removes us from the beauty of the present. Instead of receiving this beauty as a free gift, the mind starts trying to turn it into something for consumption.

I went back the next day for a repeat experience but this time, though I was again looking at the ocean and listening to the crickets, my heart was not moved in the same way. The outside 'stimulus' was the same but inside I did not have the same response. I remembered again what mindfulness teaches about unhappiness, how it arises from 'the craving for what isn't and the rejection of what is'. I concluded that a moment of extraordinary awe and wonder is not created by any particular external entity, but is more an inner, grace-filled experience, which can float naturally to the surface when we stop craving and rejecting things. It is not something we can recreate through our own willpower.

Moments of Wonder

We all have special moments in our lives – moments that lie beyond the confines of time and place. These are sometimes called moments of 'transcendence'. They are not permanent states; they are glimpses of 'intimations of heaven' coming to us, be it through a verse of poetry, a beautiful piece of music, or an inspiring sunset. While the moment is usually short-lived, we become for that time suffused with a timeless sense of wonder and awe. Whether we are looking over the city lights at night or listening to the rustling of the wind through the trees, 'one feels that life is a blessed state, that fear is unreal because death is not an extinction but merely a transition, that love surrounds and nourishes us all, and that some part of ourselves lives beyond the world of struggle and care, in the domain of pure existence'.[12]

Bliss Consciousness

In ancient India it was believed that humans are meant to experience these moments of transcendent joy, described by the Vedas as *ananda* or 'bliss consciousness'. According to Vedanta, which represents the philosophical portion of the ancient Indian scriptures, we are forever looking for our bliss, and there are a few basic reasons why we might not be experiencing it, such as the inability to recognise who we really are, identification with ego/self-image, clinging to what is transient and fear of death.

All psychology addresses, in some form, this innate longing for joy, alongside the desire to know who we really are. Freud interpreted such yearnings to be of a sexual nature, while Jung understood them as a longing for wholeness and integration. These longings are also foundational in the study of philosophy, spirituality and theology. We can spend a lifetime wrestling with the question 'Who am I?', yet we could glimpse it through one shaft of light; in an unexpected grace-filled moment. This one shining moment contains knowledge which gives us a new identity and reveals to us who we really are. However, to fully receive and remember this treasure, we may have to 'sell' something else — we may have to relinquish other identities as well as the possessive

---

12 Chopra, *Path to Love: Spiritual Lessons for Creating the Love You Need* (New York: Harmony Books, 1997), p. 93.

activity of the mind. Poet R. S. Thomas explains in 'The Bright Field':

> I have seen the sun break through
> to illuminate a small field
> for a while, and gone my way
> and forgotten it. But that was the
> pearl of great price, the one field that had
> treasure in it. I realise now
> that I must give all that I have
> to possess it. Life is not hurrying
>
> on to a receding future, nor hankering after
> an imagined past. It is the turning
> aside like Moses to the miracle
> of the lit bush, to a brightness
> that seemed as transitory as your youth
> once, but is the eternity that awaits you.[13]

The mood alteration that comes from repeated outside stimulants has quite a different texture to that which comes from an inner joy. The 'miracle of the lit bush' that the poet speaks of is transitory, yet is 'the eternity that awaits you'. It cannot be possessed or made permanent and is not found by 'hurrying on to a receding future or hankering after an imagined past'. The problem with hankering after continuous outside stimuli is that once they disappear, our happiness tends to disappear also. What's more, they often create a need for yet another stimulus, and another, sometimes leading to the dangerous ground of addiction. While fleeting pleasures

13 R. S. Thomas, 'The Bright Field', *Laboratories of the Spirit* (London: Macmillian, 1975), p. 60.

may excite, they can also anaesthetise. Mindfulness teaches us to let everything rise and fall and pass away – including our clinging to pleasant experiences. When we savour, without possessing, we are nourished and free; the burning bush is then no longer an external event, but glows and warms us from the inside – a foretaste of eternity.

Bliss of the Beloved

There comes a moment in all of our lives when we glimpse a truth we can never fully forget. This is similar to the scriptural account of the moment when the clouds parted and Jesus heard the words 'this is my son, the beloved' (Mk 9:7). One shaft of illumination became the cornerstone of Jesus' life and ministry. Because of it he was inherently free; he was free of 'the disease to please' because he carried the deepest affirmation on the inside, that of knowing his belovedness. There are moments in our lives also when the clouds in the mind part and we glimpse our belovedness. That belovedness is not something we can earn or achieve, neither is it something that can be taken from us. The freedom of knowing we are the beloved brings a fundamental relief from getting caught up in the transient. We discover that our true roots do not lie in any passing external role or public reputation but in the very core of our being.

Perhaps this is what was offered to the woman of Samaria when Jesus invited her to receive a divine inner 'spring, welling up to eternal life' (Jn 4:14). Is this an example of the 'bliss consciousness' we all thirst for? The woman had to search deeper because Jesus offered no ready-made answers; he spoke in parables, drawing her into the mystery of herself and her life, until eventually she became aware of her brokenness but also of her true nature and potential for happiness and freedom. She, and all those whom Jesus encountered, discovered something of their identity as 'beloved' and this was the foundational change. As Deepak Chopra explains, 'when you realise that your body-mind is a field of pure consciousness, then you know that you have power, freedom and grace. Therefore, happiness knows your true nature, which is all of these things.'[14]

Living in the 'Wow'

If we really knew who we were, all our relationships and all that we do would take on a new form, no longer shaped by a desperate need to win esteem or recognition. We would not be victim to every passing adulation or criticism; we could withdraw from the authority of the ego and live in the freedom of the spirit. When the clouds of doubt in our mind recede a little and we sense the truth of our own identity, we can rest in our own being, knowing that God's favour also rests on us. We glimpse something of this resting in what the mystics describe as 'love melting into love'. In this resting and melting, something softens and transforms around our perception of ourselves. We find that we no longer need to spend so much of our lives investing energy in protecting our self-image, or organising our agendas around that self-protection. We discover not just who we are, but whose we are.

This relational abiding is the place where we espouse real liberty and so are able to overcome limiting horizons; it is the place where the pulse of divine life courses through us. Consider these words by Gunilla Norris:

---

14 Chopra, *Power, Freedom, and Grace*, p. 36.

I can dwell in this home
as if it were a heart. When I feel that pulse
I know that all that comes to me will also go.
Living in this stream I understand
You are my life blood. Let me feel
You course through me, through this door
Throughout my life.[15]

A Moment for Mindfulness

1. Bring awareness to your breath, to the present moment. Notice the passing thoughts. Do not get rid of them, just note how all that comes will also go. Bring to awareness your own longing to know who you are and whose you are. When did you receive a sense of that which 'courses through you'?

2. Write about a time when you were suffused with beauty or bliss, where you felt in a blessed place, perhaps surrounded by nature, listening to a piece of music or reading poetry. Relive the experience; remember it with all your senses. Though the moment has long gone, write about how you can receive it again and recall what this experience was communicating to you. Think about how this might help you let go of the need for permanency and certainty in your life.

3. The creator of your life is reminding you that you are the beloved. Fully receive this affirmation; savour it, visualising every cell, atom and molecule of your body accepting this new identity.

---

15 Gunilla Norris, 'Locking the Door', *Being Home: Discovering the Spiritual in the Everyday* (Mahwah, NJ: HiddenSpring, 2001), p. 69.

4. A suggested closing blessing:

May I and each person I meet today,
discover that we are the beloved
and God's favour rests on us.

CHAPTER 4

Mess and Mystery:
Embracing Beauty and Pain

The mountain was steep but I was ascending quickly, passing those who were slower, trying to get somewhere more elevated, more heavenly. Mind over matter, I told myself as I climbed higher, rejecting matter in all its pain and mess. I was nearing nirvana, reaching for heaven; all the while praying 'Glory to God in the highest'. I had been keeping my focus on the upward climb until eventually I started to fall, gradually sliding downwards to a place I did not want to be, a place of damp, dirty earth. I would have continued to slide except that a hand was held out towards me. It was a scarred, weathered hand but it was firm and warm; it was the hand of one of the 'slower' climbers.

I found myself halfway down the mountain again. How I hated this in-between place. I wanted to escape. I asked God to get me back up the mountain; he didn't. I'll do it myself, I insisted. Mind over matter! Another attempt, another fall, reached out to again by that same hand – the one cut and scraped by life, covered with earth, a hand that had felt the earth and had known what falling was. If I took this hand I might be led to places I would rather not go. I might never get to the top. 'Mind over matter' I repeated as I tried to escape, only to fall a third time. Where else can I go? I asked. Surely not into those bloody, dusty, nail-scarred hands? Or into the hands of the 'slower' ones, the community of earthiness and ordinariness where there was more matter than mind. Pain and beauty, joy and sorrow co-existing, would be my companions for the rest of the journey, breath by breath, step by step, singing together, perfectly out of tune, 'Glory to God in the lowest'. I had asked for heaven but been given earth.

We might be seeking the mind but be faced instead with matter; seeking joy but receive sorrow; seeking heaven but sent earth. Jung is noted for a famous dream he had whereby he discovered the pursuit of wisdom to be a stepping downwards on a ladder. The idea of going 'downwards' is not often associated with the spiritual journey, especially as we speak of going 'up' to heaven. The ability to embrace such seeming contradictions is one of the hallmarks of healthy spirituality. Mysticism, therefore, needs to be demystified, made normal: 'that is to say where it exists in a healthy form, it appears spontaneously, as a phase in normal development; not as a self-induced condition, a psychic trick.'[16] We must ask how we can live with soul in an incarnational way, amidst the mess of everyday life. How can we balance the material and spiritual, the inner and outer, and heaven and earth with what is often referred to as the 'mastery of two worlds'. We cannot escape earth in order to get to heaven; we need to find a bit of the heaven right here, right now, just like the disciples who were asked, 'Why are you men from Galilee standing here looking into the sky?' (Acts 1:11). Jon Kabat-Zinn, author and teacher of mindfulness, advises 'to walk along the path of your own life with your eyes open, awake instead of half unconscious, responding consciously in the

16 Evelyn Underhill, *Mysticism* (Oxford: One World Publications, 1993), p. 323.

world instead of reacting automatically, mindlessly. The end result is subtly different from the other way of living in that we know we are walking a path, that we are following a way, that we are awake and aware.'[17]

On this path of awareness, we are not numbing the pain, nor are we separating it from joy; we are acknowledging that pain is part of our lives and our memories. Our past has often conditioned us to flee from painful memories, to retreat to some pseudo-positive thinking in order to escape them. We often run from what is within our own humanity. It is tempting to do this with painful memories, when all they really ask of us is to simply hold and honour them, just as they are, and not as we would want them to be. Trying to use positive thinking to avoid pain is like whistling past a graveyard. When we pause and bring a mindful awareness to what is, we are freed from resistance. Likewise, suffering is reduced when we do not add mental drama. We are then a little more disposed to embrace life and death, dark and light, beauty and sorrow.

Dancing in a Seamless Flow

We can learn to dance in a seamless flow between two partners – pleasure and pain – embracing both, yet clinging to neither. Going with the flow is like staying attuned to a background musical rhythm. When this rhythm changes we change with it; we stay attuned even if our external circumstances alter. When the dance of pleasure ends (as it will) we must bow gracefully and let it go. When the dance of sorrow comes, we must accept its offer instead of sitting it out

---

17 Jon Kabat-Zinn, *Full Catastrophe Living: How to Cope with Stress, Pain and Illness Using Mindfulness Meditation* (London: Piaktus Books Ltd,1996), p. 442.

resentfully, waiting for a happier dance to come along. Instead of contracting ourselves rigidly against sorrow and pain, we can begin to surrender to it. When we do this, we discover we are moving in harmony with a source transcending both pleasure and pain. In Buddhism this oneness is called *samadhi*, a non-dualistic state of consciousness wherein the mind becomes still and we gain insight into the changing flow of experience. Many addictions are born of the attempt to escape painful experiences and from clinging to what is pleasurable or mood altering. To try to avoid pain is a very human response; after all, even Jesus, facing his death, said, 'if it is possible, let this cup pass me by'. Yet in the next breath he surrendered his resistance: 'Nevertheless, let it be as you, not I, would have it' (Mt 26:39).

A Silver, Silent Night

The fields were covered in snow. It was the middle hours of Christmas night, 2004. The moon washed the world in silver; the roofs, covered in frost, glistened under the stars. We travelled in silence, tension filling the air. The icy roads looked dangerous, yet we had to drive as quickly as possible. We'd just had the phone call telling us my mother was very weak and we'd better come now. Apart from the faint sound of the car radio playing 'Silent Night', the world was indeed silent; it seemed asleep, unable to stay awake for this hour, this difficult hour filled with questions: Will we make it on time? Will she make it? I whispered, 'Mam, we're on the way, you are not alone, we will be there soon.' My sister was on the way too, driving on icy roads from another part of the country; my brother was also making his way on this lonely Christmas night – all of us trying to get to Mam's bedside, hoping she would be still there, minds filled with what we would say. My thoughts were interrupted suddenly by the startling ring of my mobile phone. 'Mart, she's gone … Mam is gone to God.'

The world seemed to stop breathing in that moment. There was no hurry now, the purr of the engine laboured, breathing laboured, radio turned off. 'Mart, she's gone' echoed over and over in my mind, along with questions, endless questions: 'Did she know we were all on the way to her? Did she want to wait?' Aimless, directionless, wordless, we continued the journey. 'A light gone out,' I said to myself as I stared vacantly out the window across the snow-covered fields, where my eyes rested on a light in a far-distant window. It made me wonder if there was another world beyond those silvery stars, beyond this blanket of snow, keeping the light on for Mam this Christmas night, waiting for her to come in from the cold; other voices saying, 'She's on the way!' I asked the stars about these other voices, I asked the silent moon. I looked at a frozen world, standing still in time, my own heart frozen between two worlds. A deathly silence was all that remained now, no words, just memories of words spoken and unspoken from earlier that day, last words. 'I'll be back later, Mam.' I wasn't back. I left her bedside, casting a look back as her tired eyes moved from the falling snow outside the window to the crucifix on the wall. Breathless, broken in body, perhaps she was looking at the One who knew what pain like this was, who knew what it was to be breathing your last.

Things Unsaid
Memories from Christmases past: travelling home on frosty nights long ago; the smell of ham on the boil, of Mam's potato stuffing and the plum pudding, made with her own

recipe; those times when she became like a child again. Now there would be no more Christmas homecomings, no warm potato stuffing awaiting. A journey over, no goodbye. I'm sorry that I promised I would be back, Mam. I think I knew I wouldn't be. We weren't great at saying things; we were shy about saying the important things, weren't we? I think I would say them – if I had one more day.

If there was just one more day, maybe I would help you sneak a bit more ice cream from the fridge and not spoil it by mentioning your cholesterol; I would take time to listen as you read out all those lines of poetry you had written in the little notebooks with the elastic bands around them; I would listen to what you were *not* saying; I wouldn't complain about having to repeat everything because you were deaf in your left ear. I would wear pink, even though it does not suit me, because you thought it did. There would be less silences, more cups of tea, more time for the unshed tears – all of ours; I would make more time to say the important things. I suppose I'm saying them now on this last Christmas night, a warm heart and a frozen world, sorrow and beauty wrapped for all eternity in this one silver silent night.

Sorrow and Beauty Entwined

We will never come completely to grips with 'whether the night that surrounds us is the void of absurdity and death that engulfs us or the blessed holy night already shining within us as the promise of eternal day'.[18] Questions, more questions and aching memories cloud our lives, covering them with sorrow but also lining them with silver. When I think now of my mother's death, while no less painful, there lies alongside

18 Karl Rahner, *The Eternal Year* (London: Burns & Oates, 1964), p. 80.

it memories of silver stars, a snowy moon, fields shrouded in white, a light on in a window. The night of greatest sorrow has silver linings of exquisite beauty. Bitter sorrow and sweet beauty now live beside each other, like warm plum pudding and cold ice cream. Light and shadow, accompanied with laughter and tears, presence and absence, success and failure, joy and pain. They are dancing somewhere together in all our memories.

You honour yourself and honour those who have passed on when you acknowledge how it is and how it was: messy, perhaps, not perfect, yet perfectly beautiful. As Jon Kabat-Zinn reminds us: 'If you are practicing mindfulness, then the only thing that is really important is whether you are willing to look and to be with things as they are in any moment, including discomfort and tension and your ideas about success and failure.'[19] We need to create space to bring the full texture of a person's life and our relationship to them into awareness. Sometimes, at time of burial, we hear things said like 'he was a walking saint' or some other cliché that makes us wonder if we are at the correct funeral. 'Never did any harm to anyone' or 'never said a bad word' doesn't do much to honour the full tapestry of a person's life. Such clichés do not help us to remember that those we loved and have lost were, just like us all, sometimes saints, sometimes sinners, and while they may have been unfeathered angels, they had feet of clay. In trying to canonise them, we split off the less perfect parts of our relationships, and so split off parts of ourselves. It is as if we were afraid the deceased would come back to haunt us, when the opposite is more likely to happen – that which has been split off or unacknowledged

19 Jon Kabat-Zinn, p. 442.

does the real coming back to haunt us, looking for its place, looking for the light. We must make space for mess and mystery, heaven and earth, mind and matter, beauty and pain.

A Moment for Mindfulness

1. Bring awareness to your breathing, the inhalation and exhalation. Notice how it rises and falls and how everything rises and then passes away, including what you call sorrow or joy. Bring awareness to a particular memory of sorrow in your life. Notice how you may try to get rid of it ... maybe instead you can gently hold it and create a oneness with it.

2. Move to your journal. Think of someone with whom you have unspoken words. Give yourself permission to let this exist in your awareness. Perhaps you could start writing with something like 'If I had one more day ...' Maybe you can say now what you could not say then; allow the sadness and beauty to co-exist in this silent holding place in your heart.

3. Bring your awareness and memories to the God who embraced opposites: light and shadow, death and resurrection, beauty and pain. You might be able to surrender some of those unspoken words, and receive the grace of acceptance.

4. A suggested closing blessing:

> *May I and each person be able to say:*
> *For all that has been, thank you.*
> *For all that is, amen.*
> *For all that is yet to come, yes.*

CHAPTER 5

Our Lovely Faces: The True Self

Donal was giving a presentation and was setting up a film to show to a group. He asked me to secure a laptop and projector for him. I went off to do something else and forgot. Just before the presentation was due to start, he asked where the equipment was. 'Oh, I forgot,' I said and with a familiar shame started to cover my tracks by listing all the reasons why. As I rattled off my list of excuses, I noticed Donal was smiling. When I asked why, he said, 'I wasn't even listening, I was just noticing your lovely little face.'

I like to think that at the end of time when we will be busy trying to cover our tracks while recounting our sins, we will hear those same words. In that moment, all the list of good and bad things we did in life will fall to the ground. We ourselves may fall to the ground when we see ourselves as God sees us. There will be nothing left to say except: My Lord and my God, you were gazing upon me with love all this time and I was too busy, too preoccupied, to notice how you looked at me. I was running marathons of prayers, devotions, trying to save face and trying to save myself. You were with me, but I was with a false god. So you called, you whispered. I looked up to heaven for a glimpse, I looked to holy pictures but eventually I looked in the mirror and there

I saw the shining eyes gazing back, smiling at the face you had always loved.

Eyes That See

The rich young man had real difficulty letting in that glance of unconditional love when 'Jesus looked steadily at him and loved him' (Mk 10:21). The man had hidden himself behind the compensatory self, counting what he did and what he had accumulated. He had dulled his life and spontaneity with adherence to duty. He had learnt to close down his authentic self and his human needs in order to blend into an environment he perceived could not hold the fullness of who he was. He developed his personality around having and doing and remained more preoccupied with avoiding sin than receiving grace. Perhaps, he was so insistent on calculating how much exactly he deserved that his weighing scales revealed that God owed him something, or that heaven might not be a good enough return for all the 'good things' he had done. Now, as he stood before the eyes that truly saw him, he got stuck between the longing in his soul to enter into fullness of life and the fear in his ego which resisted letting go. In counting and measuring whether the good outweighed the bad, he had missed the eyes that looked lovingly at him and invited him to enter into life.

In the stillness, we too sense the tension between the part that longs for and yet resists life. We find ourselves standing at the edge of the self, sometimes without any doorway to help us go further, and so, at some level, we, like the rich man, 'walk away sad'. However, somewhere in the stillness, we may hear the whisper that invites us to let go, where we begin to recognise something like what the poet Brendan Kennelly tells us: 'self knows that self is not enough. The deepest well becomes exhausted.'[20] We might then glimpse the shining eyes of the one 'who looks steadily at us and loves us'. In this experience of being loved, our barriers melt away; the sleeping, frightened self begins to uncoil and reach towards the light. This transformation threshold is sometimes called a *metanoia* (Greek for 'to turn around'). Some would say that loving oneself brings transformation, and while it does, we also have an infinite capacity for narcissism. We need, therefore, a mirror in which we see ourselves reflected back through the gaze of the one who beholds us. In this mirror we discover there is both the rescuer and one who is rescued, the seer and the one who is seen, the knower and one who is known. The poem in Song of Songs describes how this gaze is one which delights in us: 'show me your face, let me hear your voice; for your voice is sweet and your face is beautiful' (Song 2:14).

Ah No, I'm Fine

'If you like it, you can have it,' I remember my mother saying, adding tentatively, 'Sure you don't have a coat for the winter.' 'Ah no, I'm fine,' said the seven-year-old me, refusing the velvety red coat after I saw the price tag. 'Are you sure?' she asked, turning it over and over again, examining the lining, checking the pockets, rubbing her fingers along the soft black fur collar, holding it up, holding it out from her, looking a bit nervously at the price tag. 'Ah no, this one is fine,' I said, clutching a brown anorak I found in a bargain basket. 'We can sew on fur around the collar,' I cheerfully suggested, barely touching the hard, brown, squeaky material. I reckoned if I kept my arms away from my side and didn't swing them

20 Brendan Kennelly, 'Connection', *Familiar Strangers: New and Selected Poems, 1960–2004* (Tarset, Northumberland: Bloodaxe Books Ltd, 2004), p. 425.

too much, it wouldn't squeak so loudly. 'Are you sure?' my mother asked again, a little guiltily, but also probably a bit relieved. 'You can have the red one if you prefer it,' she said as she tentatively opened her purse again, as if checking that she had enough. I looked longingly at the pretty red coat one last time, I looked at my mother's purse and said with a stretched smile, 'Sure I don't like the colour red anyway.' I took the anorak and walked away sadly. Eventually, I pushed all thoughts of the red velvet coat out of my mind.

We can push our natural self out of awareness in order not to be 'too much'. This over-adaptation can cause us to trade authentic needs, integrity, self-worth and individuality for duty, compromise and a sad type of self-salvation. We can hide behind our having and our doing, patching and mending our lives, sewing on a compensatory self like a fur collar. We say 'Ah no, I'm fine,' to others and to ourselves, silencing the awareness of having lost our natural swing. We then begin to negotiate life according to the price tag, and when life offers to wrap us in a glorious coat of velvet, we say 'no' when we secretly long to say 'yes', avoiding the eyes that see us, even though those very eyes can become our salvation.

Remembering Where We Came From

The tendency to forget who we really are is the main cause of our unhappiness. We knew who we were when we were living in God's playground, 'by his side day after day, delighting in his presence' (Prov 8:30). We need moments to pause and remember, as the poet William Wordsworth reminds us:

Our birth is but a sleep and a forgetting:
The Soul that rises with us, our life's Star,
Hath had elsewhere its setting,
And cometh from afar:
Not in entire forgetfulness,
And not in utter nakedness,
But trailing clouds of glory do we come
From God, who is our home:
Heaven lies about us in our infancy![21]

When we become aware again that we came from 'trailing clouds of glory', we begin to chip away the layers of conditioning. That is what Michelangelo did when he was creating his beautiful marble statues and angels: he said he saw the angel first and simply cut away the marble around it. Perhaps that is what understanding our true self is: a gradual cutting away of what distances us from our God and from our joy. Thomas Aquinas is said to have suggested that God is sheer joy, and sheer joy demands company, and that we are created from the laughter of the trinity. But we often keep this God who desires our company at arms length when we remain counting the cost, trying to tell ourselves, 'Ah no, I'm fine.'

A moment of mindfulness can help us detach from the judging mind, the part which tends to continually critique and analyse good and bad, right and wrong. Some might accuse mindfulness of deleting all objective morality and bringing the dangers of 'relativism' into our spirituality. Properly understood, however, this advice to suspend

---

21 William Wordsworth, 'Ode: Intimations of Immortality from Recollections of Early Childhood', *William Wordsworth*, Stephen Gill, ed. (Oxford: Oxford University Press, 1984), pp. 297–99.

judgement is more about letting go of our own inner-judge (the false god of our own critic). In letting go of this inner rumination and self-evaluating we are free to bring all of who we are, the wheat and the darnel, under the gaze of a God who is much more merciful than we are to ourselves. Remember the prodigal son who had travelled to the distant land and experienced hunger and who, in 'returning to his senses', knew he had to 'leave this place' (Lk 15:11-32). In other words, he remembered 'the trailing clouds' where he came from, he remembered his homeland and the loving kindness of his father. Likewise, when we leave our inner home and travel to distant lands in our mind, a breath of mindfulness can lead us back to our senses. When we keep returning from those far away hills in our mind, we gradually become aware that 'our life's Star,/Hath had elsewhere its setting'. This 'elsewhere' is the place where our gaze meets God's gaze, and in that one gaze we can discover again our lovely little face.

Reminding Each Other

We need to be comfortable with where we have come from because the world will frequently remind us, as a warning not to get too big for our boots. Jesus experienced something of this reminder when it was said of him, 'this is the carpenter, surely, the son of Mary, the brother of James and Jose and Jude and Simon?'(Mk 6:3). He did not, however, let this undermine him. Rather he remembered that he had 'come from God and was returning to God' (Jn 13:3). In other words, he stayed mindful of those 'trailing clouds of glory'.

I once wrestled with the decision to give up a secure, permanent job for a way of life that I felt was more congruous with my gifts and values. I had lots of self-doubt, right up to the day I handed in my notice. On telling a work colleague that I was leaving in order to take on a new challenge, she said, 'We're not a bit surprised. Your talent for that sort of thing is written all over you.' She went on to tell me in a very affirming way about the particular gifts she and the others had apparently always noticed in me. I was grateful but also wondered why they had not mentioned these observations before now, when I was set to leave. It is worth remembering that we have opportunities every day to tell others of their 'trailing clouds of glory', to remind people what gifts are 'written all over them'.

Your Name is Written in Heaven

Saint Thérèse of Lisieux, whose path in spirituality was known as 'the little way', seemed to know a lot about mindfulness. As a child she loved to ask her father to go out into the dark night with her, to hold her hand in silence while she gazed up towards the stars. Looking upon the constellations she would say, 'See Papa, my name is written in heaven.' Such was her belief. She trusted completely that God was gazing upon her, celebrating her and delighting in her 'little way' (and her lovely little face). She saw and heard her name being called everywhere. Likewise, the great contemplative St Teresa of Ávila one day intuited that a benign presence was asking her what her name was; she replied, 'I am Teresa of Jesus.' She asked the voice who it was and she got the reply, 'I am Jesus of Teresa.' A moment of stillness awakened her, and can awaken us, not just to a discovery of who we are but also of whose we are, where in the deepest place of the heart we feel called by name and known for all eternity: 'Before I formed you in the womb I knew you' (Jer 1:5).

We might discover that we have become so identified with our job or role that we have lost touch with our essence, our real name. Any title is merely one dimension of our lives. After all, we can only bring our 'soul self' into eternity.

To be called by name is to be welcomed for the unique self that we are, not just as one of the crowd. We can detach from those things that hold up our false faces and our false names. Often, in clinging to the outside, we lose the inside. However, the more we become mindful and notice those moments of being called by name, the easier it will be at the final threshold of letting go. The Divine can break through anywhere; you never know the day nor hour when it will call your name: through a flower opening up, through a shaft of light coming through the parting clouds, through a gentle breeze blowing a rib of hair from your lovely little face.

A Moment for Mindfulness

1. Bring your awareness to your breath, to the present moment. Try to see all those thoughts as clouds passing through, and passing over. Do not try to get rid of them and do not get caught up in them. Instead, allow yourself to be anchored in the moment and in your breathing. Notice the activity of your busy mind. What does it try to protect and prove? How do you try to save face, or save yourself? What are the things that prevent you from letting in the Divine gaze?

2. Try to remember all those significant moments when your name was called. Write about them in your journal. Bring to awareness those people who have reflected back the uniqueness and gift of your own original face.

3. Listen as the Divine calls you by name. Insert your own name into this line of scripture: 'Before I formed [you] in the womb I knew [you].' Let this settle deep into your heart.

4. A suggested closing blessing:

May I and each person today
remember those 'trailing clouds of glory'
that we have come from.

CHAPTER 6

The Cover-Up:
Unbinding

I set out on my walk, breathing in the fresh morning air, reflecting on what a blessing it was to be living in the country with all its peaceful, uninterrupted walks. The more the clouds of mental activity subsided, the more the veils of separation dissolved and I felt part of everything around me; totally at one with the moment. It was late January and already there was the first glimmer of spring in the air and a spring in my step. I made my way up a secluded road, birdsong the only sound. I walked mindfully, breathing in and breathing out, noticing each step, while also being aware that I couldn't stay too long as I had to go to work soon. Taking in the full array of sights and sounds and breathing in the early morning aromas, I was filled with praise for everything that was alive and breathing. The heavy rains of the last few days had ceased and everything looked and smelled fresh; grace was pouring from everything. I was lost in the reverie of it all when a tractor came up behind me. I jumped into the ditch and the tractor sped past me, baptising me with spatters of manure as well as a generous splash from the dirty puddle in the nearby pothole. The driver waved buoyantly as he continued on his way, while I stood aghast, covered in muck. My morning mindfulness meditation quickly changed to a spontaneous mantra of profane words. I began to walk back, pounding the road in annoyance. I realised I had to be at work in fifteen minutes so I would have very little time to get back home and change. There was no longer a feeling of spring in the air. The birds no longer seemed to be singing, in fact they seemed to be mocking me with their annoying chirping. The earlier feelings of being blessed were replaced now with feelings of being cursed; feelings of grace replaced with disgrace. I muttered to myself about how much I hated living in the country with all its smelly roads and ignorant drivers. When I got home, I wiped the spatters off my clothes until there seemed to be no more muck visible. I wrapped a cardigan around me and another one on top of it, just in case. I sprayed my most overpowering perfume and rushed to work.

I had a presentation to give that day and I needed to at least look (and smell) presentable. I was still fairly new to the world of addressing large groups so it was daunting enough without having to worry about how I smelt. The opening talk went fairly well. We broke for coffee and walked towards the refreshment area, where I overheard someone say as she sniffed the air, 'Do you get it?' Her colleague twitched her nose and replied, 'Oh yeah, I do. I smell it now, it's very strong.' I panicked as I tried to walk several steps ahead. During coffee I smiled artificially and chatted while keeping a safe distance from everyone. On the way back I bumped into someone, who suddenly cupped her mouth and said, 'Oh no, I have to get out of here.' Taking this as evidence that she was about to be sick, I was just about to run after her and apologise to her for the smell when I heard her say, 'I didn't realise the time, I have an appointment and have to go now.' I was relieved but continued to keep people at a distance for the rest of the day, just in case.

On my way back to the group after lunch I noticed, to my horror, a spatter of muck still evident on my left knee. I made a quick U-turn to the toilets where I wiped the spatter furiously with a damp cloth, making it even more noticeable. I went to the hand-dryer but discovered it was too high to dry my knee. Then I was hit with a 'bright' idea: I jumped up onto the ledge surrounding the sink, balanced myself on the side of the sink, leaned my leg across to the opposite wall and arched my left knee towards the dryer. I managed to contort my body whereby one leg was now under the dryer, one hand balancing on the sink, with my heart hammering in fear that somebody would walk in and see me. I was overcome with panic when I heard voices coming down the corridor. I jumped down just before two ladies came in. Red-faced, I smiled weakly at them as I straightened myself up. I tried to reclaim some dignity and credibility as I walked towards the conference room, pulling my cardigan as far down as possible over the wet knee, which made me walk in a lopsided manner. I went back into the conference room, only to find that somebody had opened the windows.

I felt uncomfortably warm due to the layers of clothing I had kept wrapped around me, but most of all I was exhausted from the catastrophic thinking I'd been engaging in all day. Anticipating the worst, I began to read the evaluations, dreading all the criticism about the 'smelly' and 'lame' excuse for a speaker. I dreaded reading feedback from the woman who had complained about the smell at morning coffee. I dreaded what might be written by the person who had opened the window to let out the smell. Most of all, I dreaded what the two women who'd seen me acting suspiciously in the bathroom might have to say. I read hurriedly, the lines blurring, until with relief I read: 'the scones were lovely, we could smell the cinnamon from them when we went on our coffee break'; 'the room was warm and comfortable – a bit too warm so I had to open windows after lunch'. They didn't mention me at all. Of course they didn't: I had kept myself removed from them that they didn't meet *me*, only a brittle smile and layers of clothing.

Keeping Up Appearances

Looking back now, I can see how symbolic the whole mucky episode was. I had started out that day light of spirit, filled with mindfulness and awareness of the beauty of life. When I was covered in the smelly mud, I lost awareness of the blessing and allowed myself to be dragged deeper and deeper into my own 'stinking thinking'.

It reminds me of our journey in life: we come into the world, souls 'Apparell'd in celestial light'[22] and with an innate knowledge of our own beauty and the wonder around us. Then we get spattered – with hurts, criticism and rejection. Those spatters begin to define us; we become increasingly self-conscious, and the more we identify with the spatters, the more we attach ourselves to them. As children we did not have the discriminative powers to assess if other people's evaluation of us was accurate, so we took it to be our truth. We went into a kind of trance, in which we forgot our truth. In this trance, we are susceptible to any remark or criticism in our present-day lives. Whenever a critical comment comes our way, it lands on the vulnerable spot, where it resonates to confirm our unworthiness. Because we fear more criticism, we create a safe distance around us; we hide behind layers of defensiveness, armouring ourselves with titles and

22 Wordsworth, 'Ode: Intimations of Immortality'.

possessions designed to hide our sense of inferiority and shame. This armouring, we believe, will ensure that others cannot pick up our 'smell'. We spray ourselves with some artificial 'fragrance', in the form of grandiosity or superiority, in order to keep up appearances, which only serves to repress rather than heal. As John Bradshaw explains:

> The false self is always more or less than human. The false self may be a perfectionist or a slob, a family hero or a family scapegoat. As the false self is formed, the authentic self goes into hiding. Years later the layers of defence and pretence are so intense that one loses all awareness of who one really is.[23]

When we create a barrier, others lose the opportunity to truly meet us; but even worse, we lose the opportunity to meet ourselves.

The Cover-Up

In the book of Genesis we are told that we are created in the image and likeness of God. This should have put a spring in our steps, but before we even heard that good news, many influences endorsed our unworthiness and our flaws. Many of us remember being told as children that we should say an act of contrition and call to mind our sins before we go to sleep at night. How can one possibly go to sleep if they have to first call to mind their sins? This cycle of wearing false selves is where sin thrives: if I lose sight of my worth, I consequently lose sight of yours, and eventually we have to find a way to compete, fight and prove another wrong. 'Sin

---

23 John Bradshaw, *Healing the Shame That Binds You* (Deerfield Beach, FL: Health Communications Inc., 1988), p. 14.

has no kind of substance, no share in being, nor can it be recognised except by the pain it causes.'[24]

Shame itself is subtle and can only be recognised by the pain it causes. It poisons our sense of self:

> When shame is toxic, it is an excruciatingly internal experience of unexpected exposure. It is a deep cut felt primarily from the inside. It divides us from ourselves and from others. In toxic shame we disown ourselves. And this disowning demands a cover up.[25]

We are told that in the Garden of Eden they covered up by sewing fig leaves together to make loin-cloths. They hid, because they were afraid, but God called them out of their hiding (cf. Gn 3:8). Likewise, God is forever calling us from our own places of cover-up, the false self which tells us there is something fundamentally flawed about us. Through awareness, we can begin to dis-identify with the outer layers of our persona and the upper layers of the mind. This allows us to turn compassionately towards what has shamed us, instead of employing denial and pretence. Something beautiful can then begin to happen: the tightening around us begins to loosen and we start to attend to what is real; in fact, we ourselves become real.

A Moment for Mindfulness

1. Bring awareness to the breath, the rise and fall. Notice passing thoughts but do not get involved, do not push them away. Allow awareness to emerge around those outer

---

24 Julian of Norwich, *Showings*, Edmund Colledge and James Walsh, trans. (New York: Paulist Press, 1978), p. 148.

25 John Bradshaw, p. 5.

garments that you sometimes cling to, the ways you cover up and hide your true self. Do not add to these thoughts, just notice with non-judgement.

2. Write in your journal about something you can symbolically cast off, something that binds you to an image of security, power or prestige; it might be something from your wardrobe or a possession in your house. Write about what it would be like to be without it; notice your resistance to giving it away. What do you need to affirm about your worth in order to believe that you can let go of the 'cover-up'?

3. Permit memories of being shamed to come into the embrace of the Divine, allowing you to be clothed with a new garment.

4. A suggested closing blessing:

May I see beyond the outer garment of each person I meet today.
May I help to invite forth the hidden self they may be afraid to reveal.

CHAPTER 7

Childhood Mystics:
A Pearl of Great Value

His voice started out slowly and in a low tone but gradually revved up to a climax that caused everyone to sit up straight. His sermons seemed so solemn, although people didn't mind because he always said a 'fine fast Mass'. Others said that he was not well; he was suffering from 'the ould nerves'. He frequently gave harsh sermons on the commandments, especially around breaking the Sabbath by working or shopping. People half listened, they added their 'amens' and an occasional 'also with you' to the prayers, half of them heading out the door before the final blessing. Often, on passing him on the way home from Mass, the men tipped their hats and said, 'Grand sermon, Father' and went about their day. The women said, 'Are you sure you wouldn't like to call for a cup of tea, Father?', and when he declined they went for their weekly shopping. But at seven years of age, I was taking in every word, ruminating over whether I was breaking the Sabbath by buying *Bunty* or the *Beano*. I had a fairly delicate mind which seemed to cling to anything fearful or guilt-inducing and so I became more and more anxious. I already had an obsessive fear of hell and eternal damnation, and the more I feared it the more novenas I would say, trying to appease God, promising that I would improve and try harder. My health suffered and I was weak and sickly; I was often taken to the doctor, who one day suggested that maybe I was suffering from extreme tension. 'Is she afraid of anything?' he asked my mother. She shook her head; I shook my head, but wondered if maybe I should tell him about the 'hell thing'. I decided not to, thinking that maybe I too was just suffering from 'the ould nerves', so I quietly agreed to take the iron tonic and say a few more novenas.

I continued to dread going to Mass until I received my First Holy Communion, a day that felt very special. I was especially delighted to receive the gift of lovely pearly rosary beads. Each Sunday I would gaze on these beautiful beads, which changed colour depending on how the light caught them. I told myself if I focused intently on one of these pearly beads in particular, I could block out the harsh sermon and block out all my fears I had about breaking the commandments. I even believed that by focusing on the sparkling pearl, I might someday be filled with sparkle; likewise, if I focused on the angry priest, I might someday be filled with anger. So Sunday after Sunday, when the sermon started I would take out the pearly rosary beads. I imagined I could see the outline of other people in a single bead; I could see myself in it, and in this pearl we were all as one and filled with light and radiance. I began to look forward to Mass, to being lost in rapture, gazing at this precious pearl with its beautiful changing colours. At Communion time I wanted to say my prayers quickly so I could gaze at it again. I would take out the beads, say nothing, and do nothing, all my focus on the changing colours. I used to watch people coming down from Communion and wonder why they weren't smiling; didn't they know they were all shining and reflecting the light, like pearls? Maybe something in every child knows that a sparkling pearl – a sparkling God – is housed at the core of our being.

Revealed to Mere Children

Maybe it is children who truly understand what the mystics tried to tell us. Thomas Merton discovered something like the shining pearl during his epiphany in Louisville, Kentucky:

> It is like a pure diamond, blazing with the invisible light of heaven it is in everybody, and if we could see it we would see these billions of points of light coming together in the face and blaze of a sun that would make all the darkness and cruelty of life vanish completely. There is no way of telling people that they are all walking around shining like the sun.[26]

When we lose sight of the pearl within, we lose sight of it in everyone around us. This causes us to judge both ourselves and others, creating separation and division. When we focus on fear and anger we become fear and anger; when we focus on light, we become light. The years passed and I forgot the pearl of great value; I forgot what I knew then – the truth of how God gazed upon us, what oneness with God meant and what Holy Communion meant. As I left childhood behind, I also left behind this mystical awareness. As I became more adult-like and 'sensible', I forgot how to allow God to light up my colours and how to pass on that light. The pearl became a distant memory, until one day about fifteen years ago when I saw sparkly rosary beads hanging in a wardrobe of a house I was staying in. Something in my soul lit up;

26 Thomas Merton, *Conjectures of a Guilty Bystander* (New York: Doubleday, 1968), p. 158.

the sleeping child inside reawakened and began to teach me things again, reminding me of those things hidden from the sensible part and revealed to childlike hearts.

Childlike Surrender

The child knows how to surrender. This handing over our burdens to a higher source is central to every twelve-step programme for recovery, the first step of which invites us to 'name what we are powerless over', whether it be alcohol, worry, control, negative thinking and so on. The second step invites us to discover a 'power greater than ourselves for restoration'. In step three we are invited to 'turn our lives over to the care of God as we understand God'. The simplicity of this surrender takes a lifetime to embrace and is best intuited by childlike hearts.

The child can teach us how to integrate present moment attentiveness with the wonder of everything that is new, everything that is fresh. The adult mind often tries to be its own god; it makes a god of both what it is for and against; gods of our techniques and of our knowledge. We carry the defence of those gods in our strained bodies and our faces, when deep down we know we cannot do it alone. As Pierre Teilhard de Chardin tells us: 'Divine Love is capable of uniting living beings in such a way as to complete and fulfil them, for it alone takes them and joins them by what is deepest in themselves.'[27] Both the mystic and the child invite us to meet in a place beyond, where we are all one; the place habituated by pilgrims, poets and prophets; the place where the Trinity dances and invites us to join in with our own dance. In that place beyond creed, race and colour we

27 Pierre Teilhard de Chardin, *The Phenomenon of Man*, Bernard Wall, trans. (London: William Collins & Sons Co. Ltd, 1959), p. 291.

dance with otherness; we do not have to dilute our faith traditions but neither do we need to engage in the defensive for and against battles. Instead, we can open the mind, as R. S. Thomas puts it, 'so those closed porches/be opened once more ... for the better ventilating/of the atmosphere of the closed mind'.[28]

Keeping it Simple

I was wondering about some of these questions around childlikeness, mindfulness and spirituality when I bumped into Patrick. He was leaning on a gate looking across the fields. 'What are you writing about these mornings?' he asked. 'Mindfulness and spirituality,' I replied, and as I was about to continue, he interrupted: 'Ah sure things like that are lost on me. I keep it simple.' He leaned against the ditch, where his dog sat down next to him. 'What is this mindfulness about then?' he asked. I was about to explain when I decided instead to ask him a question: 'What do you do out here in the evenings?' 'Oh, I just sit,' he said. 'I like this time of the day, when the milking is finished, when the evening is folding in. I listen to the cows grazing. I just listen to all of this.' There was a sound from the sheep in the far fields. He continued, 'The sheep remind me to rest here with the shepherd when the day is over.' He began to recite a few lines of 'The Lord is My Shepherd' and I found myself joining in: 'there is nothing I shall want, beside peaceful waters ...' Patrick patted the dog's head and put his other hand into his pocket, drawing out brown rosary beads. 'Yes,' he said, 'I keep it simple. I like the feel of the beads; they keep me close to her and I remember the people I have met during the

28 R. S. Thomas, 'The Bright Field', *Laboratories of the Spirit* (London, Macmillan, 1975), p. 60.

day. She brings us all together; she brings *me* all together.' I wasn't sure who he meant by 'she'– his deceased mother, the mother of God, the maternal part of God? I didn't ask, I just sat and shared his silence and forgot to explain to him what mindfulness was.

Bringing it All Together

Patrick was, without defining it, practicing a mindfulness meditation which led to prayer and in turn led him into community – those who he met during the day. In listening to the sounds of the sheep, he was also listening *beyond* them, to the shepherd of the sheep, the silence beyond the silence. By 'keeping it simple', Patrick taught me something about how mindfulness and childlikeness have much in common; in bypassing the complexities of the mind, there is a most profound way to access wisdom. In the words of Psalm 131:

> I do not occupy myself with things
> too great and too marvellous for me.
> But I have calmed and quieted my soul,
> like a weaned child with its mother;
> my soul is like the weaned child that is with me.

A Moment for Mindfulness

1. Become aware of your breath, of your body and of the present moment. Notice the passing commentaries in your mind. Just be aware; do not add stress by adding judgements. Allow a more intuitive and bodily awareness, through the calming of the mind and all its mental chatter. You are not the chatter. Beyond and beneath the chatter there is a doorway to silence.

2. Write the answers to the following questions in your journal. What did you know as a child that you need to know again? Where was your favourite place? Through what colours did you see the world? What did you love to do as a child? Can you make space to do it in your life now?

3. Bring whatever insights are emerging, asking for a reawakening of the wonder of childlike joy and wisdom. Ask that you rediscover the mystical child in your heart.

4. A suggested closing blessing:

> *My soul is flooded with Divine light;*
> *I allow that innocent light to flow through me*
> *and to touch everyone I meet today.*

CHAPTER 8

Contemplation and Mindfulness: Similar, Yet Different

A woman rushed into the retreat house and asked me to direct her to the meditation course. I explained how there were two groups running concurrently: one on mindfulness, the other on Christian meditation. 'Oh, I don't know,' she said, 'I think a man is facilitating it.' 'Both meditations are being facilitated by men this evening,' I replied, 'so I'm still not sure which one you want.' She quickly interrupted: 'All I know is I just want meditation but I don't want the God thing!' She proceeded to attend the course she perceived to be without 'the God thing'. Her response stayed with me, leaving me wondering how the 'God thing' is sometimes perceived as an obstacle rather than an invitation to meditation. It is interesting to note how the central concepts and benefits of mindfulness are also inherent in Christian contemplative prayer.

Why would somebody want to erase God from meditation? Unfortunately, for many the 'God thing' is a corrective figure, one who reminds us of our shortcomings; certainly not one in whom we can relax and rest. This perception is sad because prayer is essentially a resting in God. We all have a longing for this resting and surrendering; perhaps that is why we are gradually reawakening and reviving the practice of contemplative prayer. It could be said that it is a practice of mindfulness which includes the 'God thing'.

Holy Longings

Modern consciousness seems to be seeking and discovering its soul and discovering that we dwell in some larger mystery which also dwells in us. Whatever name is ascribed to this mystery, people are searching for ways of praying that help, support and ground them in that search. There is a great challenge, therefore, to churches in the west to respond to the important task of assisting people in integrating conventional religious ways of praying with contemplative meditative practice.

Having trained in and explored some of the concepts of both mindfulness and Christian contemplative prayer, I can see how some people could consider them to be similar, while others question whether mindfulness can be practiced by Christians. It might be helpful to notice how Jesus embodied mindfulness when he points to a life beyond anxiety of the mind: 'That is why I am telling you, do not worry about your life, and what you are to eat, nor about your body and how you are to clothe it. For life is more than food, and the body more than clothing' (Lk 12:22-24). Jesus advises that worrying about tomorrow will not make the future better, but will only rob today of its peace. He invites us to become mindful by returning to a God-consciousness, where ordinary moments can become suffused with the extraordinary. When Jesus advises us to look at and learn from the birds of the air 'who do not sow or reap', he is challenging us to become mindful; as he does when he points to the flowers that 'never have to spin or weave'. We, however, tend to 'spin and weave' quite a bit, especially in our minds.

We get caught in the 'spinning mind' when we escape into some illusive distant future, or spin into states of worry and panic. In the east the word *saṃsāra* is used to describe this spinning. It is a word that also means 'confusion'. In other words, the overactive mind leads to confusion (a bit like the white rabbit in *Alice in Wonderland* who, going around and around in circles, ends up being late for everything). *Nirvana* is the word used to describe the more peaceful heavenly state and is considered to be the opposite of *saṃsāra*.

The practice of contemplation encourages us to be fully awake to all our experiences, neither resisting nor attaching ourselves to them – in other words, becoming free of the transitory moods, ideas or anxieties that tend to envelop us. It invites us to transcend such worry states, not merely through a concept or philosophy, but through our surrender to the loving care of a personal relationship with God.

Centering Prayer
Many of the concepts of mindfulness are evident in the practice of Christian contemplative meditation known as centering prayer. In the early 1970s, the Cistercian monk Thomas Keating noticed how many people in America were looking towards the east for meditation. At a time when contemplation was seen as appealing only to monks, centering prayer was revived through a language and method people could appreciate. I say 'revived' rather than 'developed' because it was an ancient form of prayer with roots in early desert spirituality.

Centering prayer is a prayer of silence. It takes us beyond images, thoughts and mental constructs, presupposing that some of our concepts about God can actually get in the way of experiencing God. Silence is perhaps the soul's only response to the mystery which lies beyond all our limited images and understanding. Since God is beyond anything we can define (as is our own self), words alone are inadequate to express our constant cycle of dying and rising, losing and finding and longing for home. When Jesus appeared to Mary of Magdala in the garden he said, 'Do not cling to me' (Jn 20:17). It would seem he was asking her to let go of her old way of being with him, her old images, so he could be with her in a new way, through a wordless, resurrected indwelling spring. He was inviting her to let go of their old relationship in order to make space for the new one; letting go the life that was, in order to be open to the life that could be. This non-clinging and not knowing is threatening to the ego, the part that thinks we know all about God (especially since the ego considers that we ourselves *are* God).

The main problem with thinking we already know everything is that there remains very little mystery or space for a new knowing. We have to have a 'beginner's mind' so that we can be open to what the Christian mystics describe as a supernatural knowledge which cannot be grasped by the intellect. When the disciples met Jesus after his resurrection, they did not recognise him; he was now beyond the grasp of their fixed images. He was inviting them to have a beginner's mind. We too are invited to loosen our ideas about the God we think we 'know' because it may contain much of our own projected and culturally limited beliefs. Contemplative awareness invites us to grow into the unfathomable spirit that contains the whole universe, yet exists in the core of our being.

John Main, teacher of Christian meditation, speaks of the indwelling spirit through which you 'become aware that strength comes from beyond yourself, is greater than you and contains you. Yet it is your strength.'[29] The experience of something being beyond you, yet within you, is often called 'a unitive experience'. It has been written about by many writers, such as John of the Cross: 'It seems to such a person that the entire universe is a sea of love in which it is engulfed, for conscious of the living point or centre of love within itself, it is unable to catch a sight of the boundaries of love.'[30] Unitive experiences are not reserved for mystics, nor are they the monopoly of any organisation or group; they can be experienced by any of us at a moment of grace or stillness in our lives.

Contemplative Awareness

This way of meditating does not seek to replace other methods of prayer; in fact it deepens all forms of prayer and spirituality. While in this silent state, where it seems as if nothing is happening, there can be a deep healing taking place. Your silence can symbolise a deep trust whereby instead of using language you sit in silence with the simplicity of what the centering prayer method calls a 'sacred word'. This sacred word holds your intention and your consent to rest in God's presence. Thomas Keating suggests that in this silence and consent, material from the unconscious is bubbling up to consciousness for healing. He describes this as a kind of mental detox or cleanser where the level of deep rest accessed during the prayer periods loosens up the hardpan around the emotional weeds stored in the unconscious, of which the body seems to be the greenhouse. The psyche begins to

29 John Main, *Word Made Flesh* (London: Canterbury Press, 2009), p. 17.
30 St John of the Cross, *The Living Flame of Love*, 2.10, *Collected Works of St John of the Cross*, Kieran Kavanaugh and Otilio Rodriguez, trans. (Washington DC: ICS Publications, 1991), p. 661.

spontaneously expel the undigested emotional material of a lifetime.[31]

To enable this 'loosening up' during what Keating describes as a 'deep rest', we do not chase after, engage with or suppress thoughts; we allow them to simply pass by. Any suggested postures are merely suggestions to help us compose ourselves in a receptive way, they are not a technique designed to achieve any particular result. In fact, contemplative prayer, like mindfulness, is completely devoid of any emphasis on success or goals.

Similarities and Differences

In both mindfulness and Christian meditation there is an emphasis on allowing all thoughts to pass (this includes images, insights, emotions and sensations), staying present to the breath, the present moment and the body. Some Buddhist meditation practices use the term *vipassana*, which means to 'see clearly'. When the mind wanders, we lose the ability to see clearly. However, getting annoyed with ourselves for this only increases the frustration and further prevents our ability to see clearly. Jon Kabat-Zinn in his teaching on mindfulness explains that

> while the surface of your mind can be still choppy and agitated at times, like the surface of the ocean, you can learn to accept the mind's being that way and experience at the same time an underlying inner peace in a domain that is always right here, a domain in which the waves are damped to gentle swells at most ... when you look at thoughts as just thoughts, purposefully not

31 Keating, *Invitation to Love: The Way of Christian Contemplation*, p. 3.

reacting to their content and to their emotional charge, you become at least a little freer from their attraction or repulsion. You are less likely to get sucked into them quite as much or as often.[32]

Interestingly, Teresa of Ávila provided a similar description of her own experience of contemplative prayer: 'the faculties of my Soul calmly absorbed in the remembrance of God while my thoughts, on the other hand, where wildly agitated.'[33]

Both Christian contemplation and mindfulness teach us to dis-identify with mental activity, and while they may seem similar there are distinctions: in Christian contemplation the time is intentionally dedicated and orientated to union with God. Therefore, it is intrinsically relational. There is an 'I-thou' relationship, an interplay between creator and creature, between the saviour and saved. It carries an underlying belief that God, through our consent, is actively involved and communicating with us during this time of silence. Keating goes as far as to say that God is healing and removing obstacles that prevent our full unity with the source of love. Thomas Merton tells us that

a door opens in the centre of our being, and we just fall through it into immense depths, which although they are infinite, are still accessible to us. All eternity seems to have become ours in this one placid and breathless contact.[34]

---

32 Jon Kabat-Zinn, pp. 342–3.
33 Teresa of Ávila, *Interior Castle*, 4.1, M. Starr, trans. (New York: Riverhead Books, 2004), pp. 91–2.
34 Merton, *New Seeds of Contemplation*, p. 227.

Contemplative prayer carries with it the intention to rest in God's healing presence. As R. S. Thomas reminds us:

> But the silence in the mind
> is when we live best, within
> listening distance of the silence
> we call God. This is the deep
> calling to deep of the psalm-
> writer, the bottomless ocean.
> We launch the armada of
> our thoughts on, never arriving.
>
> It is a presence, then,
> whose margins are our margins;
> that calls us out over our
> own fathoms. What to do
> but draw a little nearer to
> such ubiquity by remaining still?[35]

Perhaps if the beauty and transformative practice of contemplative prayer was reawakened more fully, there would be less hesitancy in approaching a meditation that includes the 'God thing'.

A Moment for Mindfulness

1. Begin to relax your body and breath, sitting in a relaxed but alert position. Allow a period of silence to let emerge a 'sacred word'. Dedicate this time to listening to God in the silence. When you get distracted, whisper gently the sacred word (some examples of a sacred word might be 'peace',

35 R. S. Thomas, 'But the Silence in the Mind', *Collected Later Poems 1988–2000* (Tarset, Northumberland: Bloodaxe, 2004), p. 118.

'love', 'beloved', 'Abba', etc.). Let this word rest lightly, like a feather on your heart.

2. Notice what thoughts, images, emotions surface. What might the Divine Physician be healing in your unconscious? Might there be old unhelpful images that make you want to delete the 'God thing' from your meditation?

3. Write about anything that might be an impediment to you resting, anything that is asking for healing and transformation at this time.

4. A suggested closing blessing:

> *Today, may we each recognise*
> *that the entire universe is a sea of love*
> *in which we are all engulfed.*

CHAPTER 9

Resisting and Persisting: Integrating the Body

I watched from a distance as the child screamed, her face covered in chocolate, refusing to let go of the sweets gripped in her fist. I couldn't make out if she had taken them from the shopping trolley or from the supermarket shelf. Whichever it was, she was holding them tightly, and the louder she screamed, the louder her mother screamed. 'You'll not eat your dinner if you eat those. Give them back to me!' The howling got louder until the child eventually threw herself on to the floor. Eventually, in exasperation, her mother smacked her across the back of the legs. I winced uncomfortably, wondering what would happen next. To my surprise, the howling stopped and all went quiet. In silence, the child got up and trudged along quietly, a submissive tear-stained little face, eyes averted and mouth turned downwards. The drama was over, or so the mother must have thought until she stooped over to take the bags from the trolley and received a forceful kick in the backside. I tried not to grin, until I noticed a faint but satisfied smile forming on the 'innocent' little girl's tear-streaked face.

What we try to control ends up controlling us; what we suppress will eventually rise back up and kick us in the backside. Whatever is pushed down into submission tends to come back up with an even fiercer energy. This is true whether we are talking about trying to control the bad behaviour of another person or some unwelcome trait in ourselves. In the past, the punishment system in prisons and educational and religious institutions was believed to be 'for your own good'; that harsh punishment was 'deserved'; that it would train people to behave. The kick back from that suppression is evident now; the voices once silenced are now rising up.

What We Resist, Persists

How did this controlling tendency to curb human instincts gain such a foothold? If we understand control and suppression as coming from fear, we begin to see how it gains momentum. When we fear that something may grow out of control, we often try to control it first. We don't want to own these strange, raw forces inside of us, which threaten the image we have of ourselves, so we try to whip them into shape. Unfortunately, this creates in us a tendency to whip into shape those around us also. In scripture, we encounter St Paul trying to get rid of an unwelcome force operating inside of him, one which acts against his own deeper desires: 'the good thing I want to do, I never do; the evil thing which I do not want – that is what I do' (Rm 7:19). Paul identifies something within him that seems foreign to his better self.

Sigmund Freud's psychoanalytic theory of personality refers to the ego, the superego and the id impulse. The id is unconscious and instinctive, and is driven by the need for instant gratification and pleasure. When in operation, there is an inability to delay gratification – or, in the case of the little girl described at the outset of the chapter, an inability to wait until after dinner. While the id impulse is not destructive in itself, our refusal to integrate it into our conscious life can lead it to become a destructive force: the more it is removed from consciousness, the more dangerous it is. Resistance increases tension, which further increases the power of the id impulse. It is then that our greed, rage, sloth or lack of discipline become even more unmanageable. This seriously stunts our growth and potential and explains what is meant by the flesh being at variance with the spirit: 'the desires of the spirit are in opposition to self-indulgence; they are opposites, one against the other; that is how you are prevented from doing the things that you want to do' (Gal 5:17). Understood in this way, we can see how tempting it might be to simply get rid of the id impulse, and at the very least to try to control it. However, to try to get rid of an unwelcome impulse is to engage in a losing battle because what we resist will persist.

A more mindful approach leads us to integrate and gently greet these parts, rather than repress them. In doing so, we widen our circle of compassion to include those less attractive instincts and impulses. Through becoming aware we are less controlled by these instincts. This facilitates a relationship of compassion and kindness to self and others. It allows us to accept that we are human rather than placing impossible standards on ourselves and beating ourselves up for not attaining them.

Beaten into Submission

The teenage boys arrived for the school retreat I was giving, silently, in line. Their manners were like their school uniforms: squeaky clean, impeccable. They rarely spoke out of turn; they said 'please' and 'thank you' and nodded in compliance when the headmaster gave them stern warnings about 'making the school proud' – that any less than perfect behaviour would result in punishment. 'Have I made myself clear?' There emerged a timid chorus of 'Yes, Sir'. He repeated the question louder, whereby the boys replied louder, 'Yes, Sir'. The headmaster walked away satisfied, leaving a tense silence in the room. This tension remained in the air throughout the day. The teenage boys seemed unable to express any opinions, they curbed all spontaneity and remained compliant. At the end of the day they thanked me for a 'worthwhile day'. Yet I didn't feel it had been such a worthwhile day. I felt drained from the absence of any real energy or authentic conversation in the group. When the boys left, again in a perfect line, I went to check that the building was all locked up for the evening. As I did so, I continued to think about how 'locked up' these young men had been. I wondered where they had placed their spontaneity, especially the not so nice stuff. Then I got my answer: there in front of me, written on the wall in black letters, was a display of humorous but crude graffiti – containing the headmaster's name.

The Body and Mindfulness

Warnings about the sins of the flesh have often been misunderstood to the extent where they have fostered the notion that the body is somehow bad or shameful. This has resulted in the body being deemed an impediment to spirituality, creating a dualistic, disembodied and unhealthy theology. Without an embodied approach, meditation becomes yet another form of repression. We could wear contemplative faces while denying the raw, ravenous creatures which clamour and claw under our meditation stools, but if instead we greet and befriend them, they will lie down, and snooze peacefully while we meditate. We can all snooze together and come out of the meditation more relaxed. In the practice of mindfulness meditation, the coming to awareness of passing thoughts is only one part; coming to a bodily awareness is another. Without the bodily dimension, we are in danger of suppressing what is real under the guise of detachment.

What's the Story?

A lady came to me who had just completed a mindfulness course. She had come through a really difficult experience of being treated unfairly in her workplace. When I asked her how she felt, she said 'fine' and went on to explain how she was able to 'detach' from the injustice that had been done to her because she had been taught on the mindfulness course to 'let the stories go'. She described how peaceful she felt and how she was able, through her breathing, to let all the uncomfortable, angry feelings float away, like passing clouds. When we went deeper, it was obvious that she still held deep rage under her peaceful exterior. In mindfulness she had confused the 'real story', which is held in the body, with the mental story, which is a type of mental denial. Unfortunately she had let the wrong story go. The painful account of her experience needed to be expressed, along with all the associated emotions, and not passed over 'like a cloud'. Mindfulness meditation is not meant to bypass the body but, through present-moment attentiveness, must bring us into a deeper, more compassionate relationship with it: we need to detach from the stories of the mind so that we become open to the real story in the body. We often try to escape from what we fear are dangerous emotions and bodily sensations, but these escape strategies are in fact much more dangerous.

Mindfulness, therefore, is not a kind of mental bat to fight off unwelcome sensations or emotions, neither does it reinforce or perpetuate them. Some people fear that this kind of self-acceptance could lead to self-indulgence when, in fact, it leads to integration. Instead of trying to counteract our perceived badness with controlling or rigid mental mechanisms, we allow the suppressed aspects of ourselves to come into the light of a tender, compassionate, listening presence.

A Praying Kitten

I once had a kitten called Suile. She was undersized and weak; her eyes were fearful and always watery (I think I probably called her Suile because it is the Irish for 'eyes'). I was about six, and also undersized, weak and fearful. Suile and I loved each other, but somehow I began to think that I had a job, a mission to control any unruly behaviour developing in the little cat – I had to teach her how to be good. I would place her saucer of milk on the ground and insist that she say grace before drinking it. I would join her paws together to teach her how to bless herself and try to bend her into a praying posture (I still feel guilty about that). I scolded her for not praying properly; for proceeding to drink the milk before her prayers, and for looking around her when her eyes should be closed. I spent days and hours trying to shape her into the perfect kitten. I told her she was bold, lazy and slept too much; furthermore, she continually broke the sixth commandment – she stole milk from the buckets when the cows were being milked. I thought my controlling her was for her own good. I would get very cross with her and then I would cry with guilt when I would see her watery, confused little eyes looking up at me. I would then apologise. I was in a losing battle with my Suile.

Over time, Suile's eyes got more watery, her fur lost its gloss and her body got thinner, and eventually she died before her time. I was very sad that she had passed away, but even sadder about how I had treated her. Perhaps I had done to Suile what I was doing to myself: I was bending into submission all the weaknesses and impulses that I thought were bad. I feared those parts, in the kitten and in myself, so I laid heavy burdens on both of us. Suile, please forgive me, for I knew not what I was doing.

Word Made Flesh

Descartes, in separating mind from matter, suggested that the mind or intellect is the only reliable and legitimate way of knowing anything. This could have implied that thinking about your life can somehow replace actually experiencing your life. Consequently, when an emotion is trying to become conscious, instead of experiencing it and listening to it, we would separate ourselves from it, which removes the possibility of healing. We need to replace a mechanistic and dualistic belief system with one that is holistic and embodied. Most of us were brought up with a verbal and intellectual tradition, so we did not engage the body in discerning the important choices in our lives. We have forgotten that the body is the temple of the soul, or as Jewish mysticism suggests:

> The body corresponds to the *Mishkan*, the portable temple where the Israelites worshipped in the wilderness. Our bodies can be a dwelling place for God just as the *Mishkan* was.[36]

---

36 Tamar Frankiel and Judy Greenfield, p. 38.

When scripture refers to 'dying to' or denying the flesh, it could more healthily be suggested that it become a servant rather than a master. Integrating a practice of mindfulness with an incarnational spirituality guides us towards integration of body, mind and spirit, which leads us to a compassionate God, one who became word made flesh, familiar with the human condition.

A Moment for Mindfulness

1. Relax your breathing and come back to the present moment. Allow the stories in your head to be like clouds passing over, neither getting caught up in them nor rejecting them. Perhaps you are aware of some parts of yourself that you usually try to get rid of; just bring a gentle awareness to what these might be. Now, bring a compassionate awareness to the 'real story', that which lies beneath the busy mind, the various impulses and compulsions seeking recognition.

2. What do you try to get rid of in yourself? Write down in your journal some of the sentences you use to criticise these weaknesses of mind or body. Now write how it feels to be scolded and criticised in this way. Begin to replace this criticism with an accepting, compassionate voice, one that encourages and affirms. Feel the difference in your emotions, in your body and in your energy levels.

3. Bring yourself to the awareness of the God who 'does not break the crushed reed or quench the wavering flame' (Is 42:3); one who does not see the body as an impediment to wholeness.

4. A suggested closing blessing:

*I celebrate and give thanks for the sacredness of the body,
my own and other's.
It is the temple of the spirit.*

CHAPTER 10

What Lies Beneath?: Our Need to be Needed, Our Right to be Right

Most of us, at a conscious level, seek to help and care for others and this is to be commended. However, we also need to be aware that there are unconscious forces and motives shaping what we do, influencing when we say 'yes' and when we say 'no'. No matter how important the work we do, we remain fundamentally un-free if we delete from our awareness these unconscious motives. Mindfulness should not result in the relinquishing of any of our good work, nor should it mean that we shed our responsibilities; it may, however, ask us to sift through some of the unconscious drives behind what we do and why we do it.

A number of years ago I had a responsible creative project to direct. It became quite successful but eventually I had to let it go for geographical reasons. Some time after I had left, I bumped into somebody who had been working on it with me. I asked him how the project was going since my departure. With great enthusiasm, he began to describe how much it had progressed, describing how it was 'flourishing' and going from strength to strength. To my surprise, I felt an unwelcome twinge of something I must admit was disappointment. A jealous little voice emerged from within:

'Oh, so it is flourishing … without me!' Furthermore, he didn't even acknowledge that the success of the project had anything to do with the foundations I had laid. They weren't just doing the same work as I had done, they were doing even greater work. Didn't Jesus say something about this when he had to leave his project on earth: 'In all truth I tell you, whoever believes in me will perform the same works as I do myself, and will perform even greater works' (Jn 14:12). So, I started to ruminate; round and round my mind went. 'People don't even notice that I am gone. I am not really needed. I am replaceable, dispensable. Maybe I am worthless.' The spiral continued: 'So they can manage without me? After all I did for them … all the sacrifices I made.' I had been a martyr; I had given my all and now I wasn't even missed. 'How dare they not miss me! At the very least, they could pretend.'

The Need to be Needed

Very often what we do, while innately good, is sometimes directed by motives that have their origin in the unconscious. We all need to know that we matter, that we have worth, that we are 'somebody' and that we have some measure of autonomy. If these unmet needs remain lurking in our unconscious, we may try to meet them through our roles and through those who need us and depend on us. (We can become surprisingly angry when people no longer need us or when they don't take our advice.) We need to bring these unconscious reactions into consciousness. We must do this non-judgmentally and never with self-criticism. By making space, we bring awareness to where our energy is going, allowing us to redirect it. To bring unconscious motives into the light through a mindful awareness is not the same thing as psychoanalysing them – when we allow the hidden agendas to gently surface from the basement of our minds, we can bring them to the light of Divine grace. It is only then that we can be fully open to the possibility of transformation.

However, to really receive insight into our motives we need to trace their source and understand how they are located in our personal history and upbringing. Some people try to delete memory in an attempt to become more detached and peaceful. While it is important not to replay painful memories continually in our minds, we do need to visit them if we are to be fully aware. Throughout our lives, whatever we get validation for becomes an integral part of our character. Consequently, whatever seems unworthy of love gets pushed down into our unconscious and becomes the material of our shadow. For example, if as children we picked up (either verbally or atmospherically) that always being helpful, always being right, being strong, capable and in control were praiseworthy traits, we will equate these with our self-worth and so build our self-esteem around them. By 'self-esteem', we refer, as Stanley Coopersmith explains, to

> the evaluations the individual makes and customarily maintains with regard to himself; it expresses an attitude of approval or disapproval, and indicates the extent to which the individual believes himself to be capable, significant, successful and worthy.[37]

In other words, self-esteem is a personal evaluation we hold about ourselves. It is important to recognise what may have influenced this self-evaluation; the social norms and

---

37 Stanley Coopersmith, *The Antecedents of Self-Esteem* (San Francisco: W. H. Freeman, 1967), p. 5.

significant people who held up a yardstick of what it is to be successful, worthy and so on. If we are to grow, we must look at these influences and re-examine them in the light of awareness. If the yardstick presented to us gave us the message that being vulnerable was an unacceptable way of being in the world, then we will equate being weak and uncertain as something that must be hidden, from both ourselves and others. Consequently, we begin to over-identify with what gave us esteem and reject what brought disapproval and this begins to form the basis of our persona or adapted self. If this is so, we will always be trying to achieve something that makes this adapted self feel like a 'somebody'; we will be always striving but never arriving. We notice how society frequently endorses this persona by placing a high value on success, achievement and resilience, and as a result there may be few places where we can be honest, authentic or vulnerable.

In our roles at work or in public ministry it is very easy to allow our good works to become 'gods'. Many spiritual writers – Teresa of Ávila, Ignatius of Loyola, John Cassian, Meister Eckhart, John of the Cross – warn us about the dangers of idolatry on the spiritual journey. We can create idols out of our need for control, our need to be right, attachment to our good name, over-identifying ourselves with our roles and getting our worth from the good work we do. These attachments begin in the mind, and according to Eckhart, we must keep

a watchful, honest, active oversight of all one's mental attitudes towards things and people. It is not to be learned by world-flight, running away from things, turning solitary and going apart from the world.

Rather, one must learn an inner solitude, where or with whomsoever he may be.[38]

We all wrestle with the opposing needs of our ego and of our spirit, and they are often at variance with one another. It is crucial that we are always aware of their subtleties and of how their voices differ. Somebody once told me that she regularly asks herself this question: Do I want to be right or do I want to be well? The ego will always want us to be right while the spirit will always want us to be well. Knowing the difference between ego and spirit is integral to living mindfully. The voice of the spirit is like an 'aha' moment: it is fresh, intuitive and uplifting; it challenges but never shames; it does not force or control but, like the wind, it 'blows where it pleases; you can hear its sound, but you cannot tell where it comes from or where it is going' (Jn 3:8). In the presence of the Spirit, even though you cannot tell where it comes from, you notice a sense of expansion and lightness, an enthusiasm for life. Following the dictates of the ego, on the other hand, creates contraction, rigidity and control.

The Need to be Right

Voices were getting louder, fingers starting to point, eyes narrowing, arms crossing. We were all locked into trying to prove who was right and who was wrong. We were at a meeting to discuss advocacy issues concerning the unheard voices of some children with special needs. The focus had subtly shifted; no longer arguing on behalf of the children, now it was which of our own voices would be heard and would win the argument. We backed up persuasive arguments

38 Raymond Bernard Blakney, ed., trans., *Meister Eckhart: A Modern Translation* (New York: Harper & Bros, 1941), p. 9.

with proof of how right each of us was, and consequently how wrong everyone else was. Folders were opened, various official documents and even Bible quotes were cited, each of us trying to sound more persuasive than the other. Like boxers, eyes glared as we prepared for the fight; tension rose. Eventually, the bell sounded (in the form of coffee time being called). During the break we went into clusters on opposite sides of the room; huddles formed as our 'coaches' advised us on what we needed to do to win the second round. The meeting resumed and we were back in the ring. Whose opinion would win before the final bell? Of course it wasn't actually terminated with a bell, but with a closing prayer. The time was up, the meeting was over and during the closing meditation the air remained thick with conflict, evident in voices, clenched fists and agitated sighs. The person leading the meditation invited us all to relax and breathe. After a few moments of stillness, I noticed my own fists starting to uncoil; my toes straightened out from their curled position. I closed my eyes for a while, calmed my breathing, and when I opened them again I saw some of the other attendees still glaring at one another across the room. Nobody wanted to let go of their opinion. In the silence, I began to notice a faint nervousness behind the glares of some; in others I just saw a more vacant look, something that resembled sadness. The angry fronts seemed now more like a plea: 'I'll prove to you that I am somebody. I'll make you respect me.' My eyes were drawn to one person in particular who had a rash visible all the way up to her elbow. I noticed the fear in her eyes. Folders lay on the floor, like surrendered arms on the battlefield. Briefcases filled with persuasive arguments now lay on laps. Name badges hung redundant on jackets. I met the eyes of some of the others; they met mine. When I blinked I thought I felt an unwelcome moisture in my eyes: the discomfort of holding back that emotion reminded me that I wanted to be 'well rather than to be right'; in fact, for all of us to be well regardless of who was right. In the argument we could not hear one another because we were all planning what we would say to defend ourselves. Even the coffee break did not interrupt the rising tide of reactivity; it had continued to bubble under the surface. It was only now, in the silence, that the emotional charge dissipated; the breath of awareness broke the stories in our heads.

In the silent moment of mindfulness, we are transported to a place beyond right and wrong; a place where our most dominant defences can subside. A return to present moment attentiveness facilitates an enquiry into what we do and why we do it, a moment that demonstrates to us the senselessness of needing to be right.

In trying to make decisions that would affect the lives of children, we had all got embroiled in our own unmet needs – the place where all our wars start. This is where 'righteousness' is born; it eventually blinds us and prevents us from seeing the truth. If we give in to it then it becomes insatiable and generates even bigger wars. When we pause, breathe and look with softer eyes, even for a moment, we create a space for something else to emerge: a deeper moment of insight, what Buddhists call *prajna*. In this moment we can discern that barely audible voice: the whisper of the spirit. In ceasing to make the other into the enemy, we face two opposing choices: our ego wants to continue to defend our self-image, while our soul, aware of some larger reality, wants to connect. This 'larger reality' is also described in the Buddhist philosophy as *drala*, which means a harmonious place beyond the enemy. In that space we can connect with our own inner wound and the wound in the other. Rainer Maria Rilke tells us that when people let go of these defences, 'a wonderful living side by side can grow up, if they succeed in loving the distance between them which makes it possible for each to see the other whole and against a wide sky'.[39] By way of this 'wide sky' we see and find compassion; we might even learn to 'love the distance' between us. We also get a glimpse of what is driving our habituated need to be right, usually located somewhere in our early life. Through this deeper understanding, the antagoniser loses face and becomes somebody very small. This somebody small is in me and in you, simply asking 'please see me behind my armour, please see my desperate attempts to prove that I am somebody, please don't tell me that I am nothing. Even if I hurt you with my tight fists, please see me. I am more like you than you realise. I am afraid just like you. I, too, am a child.'

Transfer or Transform

We are all born with the basic need to survive, to have esteem, to have control. If there is a lack, or perceived lack, in any of these areas we will go looking for them to be met unconsciously. We look for some replacement to give us an escape from having to look at the more difficult parts of our nature; we can try to control and fight the outer, whilst never addressing the inner. When we become mindful, allowing enquiry into what is shaping our actions, we are able to step out of the ring. The whole dynamic changes by stepping back. It takes just one mindful person to stop a fight, maybe even a war, in its tracks. When our own fight to be right

39 Rainer Maria Rilke, *Rilke on Love and Other Difficulties: Translations and Considerations* (London: W. W. Norton & Company, 1994), p. 34.

dissolves, our own suffering dissolves. We transform, rather than transfer, what lies beneath.

A Moment for Mindfulness

1. Relax your breath and come to present-moment attentiveness. Notice not just outside sounds but inner clamouring: perhaps inner-strivings to be right, to be in control. Simply notice your need to be right; be aware of what you do, how you do it and how this affects your body, then return your focus to your breathing.

2. Write in your journal about the times when there may have been another agenda in charge. Try to uncover what forces were pushing through from the unconscious. How might your need to be needed, your need to be right or your need to win have been operating below the surface? Is there a way you tend to make others dependent on you? Why and when did you learn to do this? Write about what these things are, bringing them to the light of awareness.

3. Bring to prayer the memories that drove you to find your esteem in battles with others. Allow yourself to lean into the embrace of God, who knows your story and your need to be right or in control. Rest like a child whose story is heard and held.

4. A suggested closing blessing:

Let there be light:
light in my conscious self,
light in my unconscious,
and light sent to everyone I meet this day.

CHAPTER 11

Train of Thought:
Selling our Peace

I recently treated myself to a first class train ticket. I looked forward to enjoying some peace and quiet on this Sunday morning – which I did for the first forty minutes, until my peace was interrupted by the sound of rattling bags being placed on the table in front of me. A woman shuffled on to the seat beside me, her phone to her ear: 'I have some free minutes, so I decided to use them up by ringing you.' Phonecall after phonecall, the woman loudly shared a number of gossipy stories. As she did so, each precious moment of what could have been a tranquil journey was disrupted. Eventually, the train began to slow and I heard her say, 'Oh, I'll have to go now. My stop is coming up and I want to get twelve o'clock Mass when I get there.'

My first class experience was not as peaceful as I had anticipated, but it did give me a first class reminder about all the ways we can mindlessly break the commandment 'Thou shalt not kill'. We do it with our words, our mindless gossip, which can kill the character of another. After the woman had disembarked I began to question all the times I had gone to Mass without thinking about what I'd done to desecrate the body of Christ in my 'free minutes'. I wondered what it would be like for any of us if on approaching the altar we heard the words, 'This is my body, this is my blood' and recognised it was the same body we were gossiping about earlier. As a result of that Sunday morning experience, I am more mindful of my own 'final destination', where I might come face to face with someone whose character I had once called into question.

Scripture advises us that 'a flood of words is never without its fault, he who has his lips controlled is a prudent man' (Prov 10:19). Likewise the Buddhists remind us to be loving in our speech: 'I am determined not to spread bad news that I do not know to be certain and not to utter words that can cause division or discord.'[40] Mindfulness helps us choose the words we utter carefully; to understand whether they have the potential to nourish or poison. This extends to the words we choose to listen to.

Perhaps we can only truly free ourselves of our tendencies to judge the weaknesses of others by cultivating a tolerance for our own weaknesses. When we berate ourselves for not living up to our idealised self-image, we tend to berate others in turn and consequently lose our peace. So often our hardening of heart can be halted if we stop the morass of self-criticism before it spirals out of control. It is through the lens of self-condemnation that we begin to condemn others. Scripture advises, 'let your behaviour change, modelled by your new mind (Rm 12:2). This 'new mind' has to be cultivated because the damage of old habits is hard to undo. However, when we begin to become mindful of autopilot spirals of negativity, we create space around them; we are then free to create new thought patterns.

---

40 Thich Nhat Hanh, *Peace is Every Breath: A Practice for Our Busy Lives* (London: Ebury, 2011), p. 144.

The Downward Spiral

It was the beginning of Lent and Anne had promised to cut down on coffee and chocolate (her favourite indulgences). She also had the intention of getting up earlier each morning to spend more time in meditation and had vowed to resume her daily walk. Ash Wednesday arrived – the first day of her new regime – and she woke early to the sound of the alarm. Her good intention of getting up early flashed through her mind but was soon forgotten as she buried her head deeper into the pillow and went back to sleep. Much later, already annoyed with herself, she crawled out of bed and had a strong coffee. Anne decided there was little point in doing meditation now. With all her motivation gone, she felt exhausted and ate a few squares of chocolate 'for energy'. She left the house, forgetting her shopping list. As she tried to remember what was on it, another list entered her head – a catalogue of self-criticism: weak, lazy, disgraceful, incapable of keeping promises. The queue in the supermarket was long and the checkout closed just as she was approaching. Waiting in another line, Anne noticed a magazine with the headline 'Take charge of your life'. 'I'll take charge of it tomorrow,' she told herself. Leaving the supermarket, Anne drove past some women jogging and turned her annoyance outwards, muttering how ridiculous they looked, fuming at how much of the road they took up. 'Why am I being persecuted?' she asked, beeping her horn at the joggers.

Admitting the 'Think' Problem

For Anne, the problem did not begin when she indulged her desire to stay in bed a little longer. Rather, the problem began when she allowed herself to indulge in self-critical thinking; the negative stream of self-scolding that descends into a spiral of negative thoughts. Like attracts like, and before you know it you are in a bad mood; you have crushed your own spirit. When you grant these thoughts the authority to determine your own peace, you lose your present-moment attentiveness. Even pausing for a single breath could interrupt the build-up of this escalating spiral of self-criticism.

It can be liberating to discover that just because you have a thought, it doesn't mean you have to think it. The first thought is the one to catch; that is the time you can decide not to continue with it. For people with alcohol addiction, there is no such thing as 'one drink'; the first drink leads to another, and then another. When we indulge in the 'first think', it nearly always leads to a second and a third, until we become drunk with negative thinking. Anne felt persecuted but imagined that it was others who were to blame, when she was actually attacking herself.

Such persecutory agitation does not just affect us just for one day; it remains with us, a sort of 'thinking hangover'. A moment of mindfulness can prevent this. By noticing and naming the mental states we are experiencing, we can halt them before they take over. This self-awareness is not to be used as a way of further persecuting ourselves; awareness without compassion can amplify our shortcomings, adding another layer of self-criticism. The noticing and naming must be accompanied by a compassionate understanding of where this persecutory tendency comes from. A person with a drink problem will not find sobriety solely by becoming aware of their problem: they must also surrender and, as the eleventh step advises, 'through prayer and meditation seek to improve conscious contact with God'. Surrendering to a higher power is also necessary in changing our thought patterns. Pasting over these negative thoughts with positive ones can work to a certain extent, but we have to identify long-term practices for dealing with them. A practice of mindfulness integrated with a spirituality of surrender helps us deal with the think problem.

Persecutory Anxiety

Psychoanalyst Melanie Klein, one of the leading innovators in object relations theory, describes how from childhood we split off 'bad' feelings and project them outwards, causing paranoia and a sense of being attacked (emotionally or otherwise). Taken to its extreme, the 'persecutory other' becomes the attacker. This projection may cause us to enter into a spiral of negative thinking about how others are looking at us and talking about us. 'Catastrophising' is the term used in mindfulness to describe these mental imaginings. When we feel victimised and hard done by, our negative mood tends to attract and gather other negatives and we find ourselves in persecutory prisons of our own making. A few seemingly harmless thoughts at the beginning of a day can have a gravitational pull towards a whole host of other undesirable states. It is as if when we leave our windows or doors ajar we are inviting the thief to break in and steal our peace. Our greatest riches – joy, peace, self-esteem, integrity – can be taken from us when we leave ourselves open to negativity, our own or that of others.

The first step is to bring a moment of mindfulness to what we are doing; the second is to bring openness to understanding the root cause of this persecutory pattern; the third is surrender. Like those who must admit their difficulty in managing their drinking and then surrender to their problem, we have to acknowledge our difficulty in managing our thinking and surrender. In this way, the first murmur of gossip, the first time we skip exercise or the first piece of chocolate can be an opportunity to find compassion for our human weakness. When we pile unreal expectations on ourself or others, we set the stage for disappointment. When we ease up on our list of shoulds and should nots we are less likely to become intoxicated by that 'first think'.

A Perfect Saturday Evening

There are many Saturdays when I reluctantly leave the house to go to work, thinking the rest of the world is enjoying a lie-in. These mornings are sweetened a little by the prospect of coming home in the evening and reading the paper by the fire – the house hopefully cleaned in my absence. On leaving the house I remind Pat to pick up the paper. I don't ask him to clean the house but admit I have, on more than one occasion, placed the vacuum in a prominent position, the lead stretched across the hallway so he can't miss it. One such Saturday, as I was driving home, thoughts filled my mind: 'Pat better have remembered to buy the paper and light the fire. I hope he noticed the vacuum cleaner in the hallway.' I told myself that if all these expectations were met, I could relax and read the paper. As I turned the corner I saw smoke coming from the chimney: one thing ticked off. As I came in the back door, I could smell something cooking: great, this was shaping up to be a perfect Saturday evening. 'Come on, darling. Come and have your dinner.' As I made my way eagerly towards the kitchen, my mind conjured another list of expectations: flowers, wine, dinner on the table. I walked in to find Pat kneeling on the floor, holding out a bowl of food to our dog, Holly. He eventually noticed me standing there and said, 'I've just put on toast. Would you like a slice?' He sat down at the table, buttered a slice of toast for himself and proceeded to stretch the paper out in front of him. Silence descended, except for the occasional sound of crackling from the fire and the chewing of toast. I looked around and noticed the vacuum cleaner stationed in exactly the same position I'd left it. What had he been doing all day? I looked for evidence: the TV guide opened on the sofa. Tired, I sat down on the couch and started dozing off, only to be woken occasionally by Pat's giggles, 'Listen to this …' 'I can read it myself later,' I interrupted. Silence descended again. Another part of the paper lay on the floor, while Holly had the weekend section in her mouth. Eventually, Pat took it from her and asked me if I wanted to read it. 'Ah, no I'm too tired now, I'll read it tomorrow, it's late now. Besides I have to *vacuum the hallway.*' As Pat got up, I noticed he was limping. 'It's nothing,' he said, 'I tripped over the lead of the vacuum this morning and my back isn't great since. I had a list of chores I wanted to get done today too.' I look away and said, 'At least you got the paper.' Guiltily, I wound up the lead of the vacuum cleaner up and put it away in its rightful place. I looked at Pat as he turned out the light, while another light went on in my awareness and I thought to myself: expectations trip us up. I asked God to show me how to let go of those fixed expectations about what constitutes perfection.

We need to have a daily practice of noticing those thoughts and mindsets that are filled with expectations of perfection – perfect Saturdays, perfect houses, perfect people – and how they create 'dangerous leads', which lead us away from peace and from the gift of this 'perfect' moment, just as it is, right here and right now. Certain things disconnect us from peace; amongst them are our expectations of how others should be, how life should be, how we should be. They lead to disappointment, self-pity and ingratitude; they don't just trip us up, they trip up those around us. Our expectations of how things should be can turn the present moment from heaven into hell.

When the mind goes into default mode, as it does regularly, we find ourselves disconnected from the present moment. Expectations, as such, are not the problem, it is our attachment to them that lures us into illusory notions of perfection. We can, however, begin to dis-identify with these mental projections through awareness; to return to the right here, right now. In the present moment there is always a homecoming party awaiting us.

A Moment for Mindfulness

1. Bring awareness to your breath, to present-moment attentiveness. If you are caught up in anticipation or expectation, just notice this and come back to your breath and senses.

2. Draw a line down the middle of a page in your journal. On one side, list those states that might create 'dangerous leads' – those attitudes and habits that pull you away from the present moment and 'trip you up'. You might identify them as control, regret, self-pity, judgement, resentment, self-criticism, and suchlike. On the other side of the page, list what you can do to counteract the 'first think' of the day – attitudes that are life-giving, such as trust, gratitude, self-acceptance and kindness. Keep this list with you as a type of inventory for reference throughout the day.

3. Ask your higher power to show you how to recognise the unmanageability of negative thinking in your life and to learn how to surrender before the 'first think' begins to kidnap your peace.

4. A suggested closing blessing:

*Today I will create a heaven
where my mind tries to create hell.
I desire this heaven for everyone I meet this day.*

CHAPTER 12

The Banquet:
Mindfulness and Abundance

All religions advise us to prioritise the higher things, those of the spirit. 'Set your hearts on the kingdom,' the gospel advises us, so that 'all these other things will be given you as well' (Mt 6:33). This suggests that if we search for interior freedom, for a way of life that nourishes our souls individually and collectively, the rest will flow more naturally. No longer clinging, controlling or hoarding things, we then have the capacity to be rich or poor, yet defined by neither. We may all dream of a life with plenty, but it is said that once we move beyond poverty, further economic gain does not provide a sense of abundance. Sometimes we are told that the poor are closest to God; I think that is true only if we consider 'poor' to also mean poor in spirit, poor in disposition. Mindfulness teaches about non-attachment, which is not about having or not having but more about not being bound to the things we do have or hankering after the things we do not. Inner freedom doesn't automatically accompany material poverty; we have all met people who are materially rich and also open in spirit, generous and humble. Likewise, we have met people who own very little of the world's possessions but are abundantly rich in their attitude and in their spirit. There are people, some of whom are rich and some poor, who carry a sense of scarcity or deprivation and are unable to let go the 'hard done by' complex. It is not how materially rich or poor we are but the attitude we espouse that determines our feelings of abundance. As St Paul said, 'I know how to be poor and I know how to be rich too. I have been through my initiation and now I am ready for anything anywhere; full stomach or empty stomach, poverty or plenty' (Phil 4:12). Inner freedom, therefore, is not so much about what you possess but about what possesses you.

Hoarding, hiding and accumulating is usually based on some underlying fear. This fear can cause us to create a compensatory security; one that we think will shield us from having to depend on anyone for anything. Our life can become an obsessive pursuit of acquiring and grasping more and more stuff, imagining this will bring us security, whereas it is in losing our grasp on life that we actually find it.

Just a Little Bit

I remember a conversation I had long ago with an elderly nun. She was small in stature, fragile, saintly looking. She fidgeted nervously as she spoke and looked as if she needed a hug or some reassurance. She was wistfully recalling the journey of her life in the convent, the vows she had taken – poverty, chastity and obedience – and the different challenges she met in living her vocation. I felt sympathy for her, in what seemed like her tendency towards scrupulosity. She went on to explain how she had 'a little bit of money', which she had never told the religious congregation about. 'Just a little bit,' she repeated. 'I suppose I should have said something about it but it just never came up.' I interrupted by advising her that maybe she need not worry about that 'little bit' of money, assuring her that God was probably delighted she was able to be in possession of something that was just hers.

I asked her if she had bought anything nice for herself with it. I suppose I wanted to console this elderly, fragile little nun who seemed to be not of this world. As she pondered my question, her eyes narrowed wistfully and eventually, after a long silence, she began to answer tentatively: 'Well, yes, I did buy something. I bought ... well, you see ... I actually bought an apartment.' Before I had time to be shocked, she continued to explain where the apartment was – in an exclusive, upmarket location. I did not know what to say. The nun broke the silence by adding in a barely audible whisper, 'I suppose I should have told the order about the little bit left over, but sure there is really no point now.' She paused again and with a sad, faraway look in her eyes, which I thought might be remorse, she said, 'No, there's no point now. It is too late because it is all invested in shares.' She fell silent again and with a heavy sigh continued in a more defiant tone, 'Yes, unfortunately I invested in shares and sure now they've all gone belly up.' I stared incredulously at this saintly little woman, fragile in body but feisty in spirit.

Freedom of the banquet does not come with belonging to a specific religion or congregation or organisation; it doesn't come through a position or even a set of beliefs. We can haul a spirit of scarcity and hoarding across the door of a religious institution as much as across a financial institution. Freedom of the banquet neither comes with material poverty nor material richness, rather it comes from a spirit of abundance – a heart which is able to be rich or to be poor while remaining defined by neither. This type of disposition is not a one-off choice we make in life but more a constant daily growing into an awareness of what it is to live in freedom, where each day offers us moments to choose or refuse this banquet. The word 'banquet' denotes living with a certain kind of consciousness that leads to abundance and generosity. When we refuse the banquet and choose to hoard and hold our riches in a possessive way, we are not living in a spirit of abundance but in a spirit of fear. This fear gives us a sense of scarcity, no matter how many bank accounts or apartments we possess. 'If you make a list of everything you own, everything you think of as you, everything that you prefer, that list would be the distance between you and the living truth.'[41]

A Forbidden Heaven

I loved that big whitewashed house, the one with what looked like a secret garden and orchard at the back. It was like something from a storybook; roses growing up around the half door, a cat stretched out lazily at its entrance. It looked like a little bit of heaven. It was right next to one of the hayfields we had rented, so I often gazed over the ditch imagining who might be living there. I was about seven years old so, even though it was only a cottage, the house looked huge to me. One day I climbed the ditch and I pressed my face against the window; I saw an old man smoking his pipe leisurely by the fire. I ran back to the hayfield to tell the busy adults about the lovely house. My excitement was cautioned with, 'Ah, but people in big fancy houses will never get to heaven. Easier for a camel to get through the eye of a needle …' Added to that was a reminder that 'The devil finds work for idle hands'. Many days afterwards, I pressed my face against the window again. I watched the old man smoking his pipe and my heart was filled with sadness, picturing this plump little man trying to get his belly through the eye of a

41 Stephen Levine, *Who Dies?: An Investigation of Conscious Living and Conscious Dying* (New York: Doubleday Publishing, 1982), p. 182.

needle. I wondered if I should knock on the glass and warn him that he would never get to heaven or that the devil would get at his idle hands if he didn't start working fast. Maybe it was there and then I decided I would not get to heaven either if I allowed myself beautiful flowers or any other nice things in life. That made me sad, and I suspect it made God sad too.

Heaven Without Flowers

I once received a beautiful bunch of lilies unexpectedly. I decided I would put them in the chapel for everyone to enjoy. After all, if the choice was between flowers or heaven, I reckoned I'd better say no to the flowers! I put them, still wrapped in their plastic, in the car the following morning – and forgot about them. A couple of days later I saw them on the back seat, wilted, drooped and withered. As I tried to clean the stain the pollen had left on the seat, I began to wonder why my ability to receive was so drooped and withered.

In India, they advise us to live by *dharma*, which means to 'live by grace'. Living by *dharma* is also what Jesus calls us to when he says to trust in providence (cf. Lk 12:22). When we live in this flow of grace, our lives feel abundant. Sometimes the most difficult thing is to receive, especially when there is no possibility of being able to give back. Who knows, maybe we can have flowers and heaven too.

Paying for Happiness

The idea that we have to pay for our abundance can live on in the psyche somewhere. We might notice that we put all sorts of criteria in place before we allow ourselves something nice. 'Deserving' is a dangerous concept because we will devise all sorts of reasons why such and such a person deserves, and why someone else does not. Another contributing factor to our guilt around deserving comes with too much emphasis on 'the good old days'. I remember hearing adults talk about how they only got an orange for Christmas, how they walked miles to school in all weather and shared the one pair of shoes between them. These stories never inspired me to be more grateful. When we make too much of a virtue of having to do without or of 'hard times', it can make us mean-spirited and judgemental of those who seem to be having too good a time.

When we stop focusing on our own earning or deserving, we discover a space in our lives. In Buddhist philosophy, the term *shunyata* describes a certain type of emptiness, where nothing has an intrinsic existence in itself and nothing has permanency. This empty place is also the place where we can be open to receiving. There are places in our minds, hearts and psyches that need to be empty so that we can receive back the expansiveness of life; where, through that emptiness, we experience 'the largeness of life that now lies open to our souls'.[42] Many forces in the world insist that we fill our emptiness with an achieving energy, which can take over our lives. We can have a compulsion towards filling empty spaces. We hang an image or an ornament on every blank wall and empty space of our lives, when those very spaces could bring us into a spirit of serenity and receptivity to the overflowing gift of breathing in and out in the present moment.

When is Enough Enough?

Good Friday, traditionally and still for many, is a day of silence and fasting. The night before Good Friday last, I saw quite

42 Parker J. Palmer, *Let Your Life Speak: Listening for the Voice of Vocation* (San Francisco: Jossey-Bass, 2004), p. 54.

a number of people at the supermarket checkout, trolleys filled with food and drink. There was an air of panic; it was as if people were stocking up, trying to fill the emptiness of Good Friday at all costs: we better have enough in the house, just in case. We act in a similar way on a daily basis – filling up and accumulating, just in case.

There are many people whose goal is to become financially secure, forcing them to stay on treadmills of accumulation that exhaust them. They argue that financial security brings abundance. Some say that 'having enough' can give peace of mind, but could it be that it is peace of mind which brings a sense of having enough? We can become so conditioned to accumulating and earning that we lock up that part of our heart which has the capacity to receive and to experience the spirit of abundance. We can feel a temporary satisfaction, even a 'high' when we deny ourselves this abundance; we can even feel a little bit superior to those who are so self-indulgent. If we are withholding towards ourselves, we are more likely to be withholding towards others also. We might fear that being the recipient of another's generosity will give us an out of control feeling; this can be uncomfortable if we have always prided ourselves on self-sufficiency and avoided being indebted to anybody. If we see the world not as abundant but as perpetually adversarial, we might fear that what we have could be taken from us. We often refuse life's little moments of abundance in order to retain our sense of control and apparent self-sufficiency.

Receiving or Grabbing

My dog, Holly, gets very excited when she sees the box of dog biscuits coming out. Just the sound of the box opening has her twirling around and jumping up and down. She makes yelping sounds, and then the anticipated moment arrives: I hold out the biscuit and my fingers are nearly snapped off. I sometimes think I must have dropped it, because I do not see or hear any sound of chewing. All I see are two big hungry eyes looking up at me begging for more. The same thing happens with the second biscuit: again, no chewing, just one loud gulp and both the biscuit and the moment is gone. I find myself saying, 'You didn't savour it, you didn't even taste it.' In this, Holly reminds me of how sometimes we too, in our fear of there not being enough, grab instead of savouring. To grab is to believe in scarcity, to savour is to believe in abundance.

No matter how much of the world's goodies we grab, we remain empty, hungry and begging for more; whereas when we receive, taste and savour with mindfulness, we feel abundantly rich and nourished. Life's pleasures are then no longer outside and passing but are interior, deeply felt experiences which continue to nourish us long after we have digested them.

A Moment for Mindfulness

1. Become aware of your breathing – fast or slow, shallow or light. Do not change it, just notice it. Notice your body, especially those areas of tightening or holding, clenched fists and closed arms. Just notice and name without judgement. Bring awareness to how familiar that pattern may be, how long you have been holding on, earning or hoarding.

2. When did you first start fearing scarcity? When did you first fear that there might not be enough? What did you do to try to ensure plenty? In your journal, write down whatever comes to you in answer to these questions.

3. Bring your fear of scarcity into the awareness of an abundant higher power who has a banquet awaiting you. Ask for a glimpse of the banquet so that you may hold it in view, especially on those days where you worry and fret about scarcity.

4. A suggested closing blessing:

May I, and each person,
notice the free gifts of Providence.
May we learn to receive rather than grab them this day.

CHAPTER 13

The Crash:
Slowing Down

I was driving from one event to another, rather pleased with how much I had achieved that day. 'Three more busy weeks and I will have saved up enough time off for Christmas,' I thought to myself. All rest and recreation was postponed until the Christmas holidays, and I filled my days with ticking lists and getting things done. 'I must up the pace now,' I told myself as I increased pressure on the accelerator while throwing a sideways glance at a spectacular flashing Christmas tree in the front of someone's lawn. Next thing I knew, I had rammed into the back of the car in front of me. An hour later, whiplash collar on my neck and red-faced, I tried to explain to the doctor how I had rear-ended a car while looking at a Christmas tree. The doctor laughed and tried to console me by telling me of a similar incident when a poster advertising nylon tights on a street corner had caused *him* to crash.

We should not have to crash to discover the price we pay for the fast pace of our lives. When our attention is divided, our concentration and vision become obscured and we lose the ability to notice life's more tender beauties, especially those in nature, poetry, art and music. A life taken over with busyness can result in the things of the spirit being forgotten. Stephen R. Covey, author of *The Seven Habits of*

Highly Effective People, differentiates between the urgent and what is truly important. He suggests that we could spend all our lives putting out fires and saying 'yes' to every urgent demand, while never living out the deeper values of our core selves:

> Keep in mind that you are always saying 'no' to something. If it isn't to the apparent, urgent things in your life, it is probably to the more fundamental, highly important things. Even when the urgent is good, the good can keep you from your best; keep you from your unique contribution, if you let it.[43]

Jesus said something similar to Martha, who was busy with so many things, when, according to him, so few are necessary. In other words, much of what we call 'urgent' is not as important as we think. He points to Mary as one who has chosen to attend to the important rather than the urgent. This is challenging, as the urgent nearly always presents itself as being the right thing to attend to. Covey says we must discover our deepest values, which come from 'striking at the root – the fabric of our thought, the fundamental, essential paradigms, which give definition to our character and create the lens through which we see the world'.[44] Again, in the gospel we hear the same idea, when Jesus addresses Martha: 'few are necessary, indeed only one' (Lk 10:42). An inordinate clinging to the urgent can keep us forever embroiled in diversionary tactics, thus preventing us from being free to accept the invitation to the banquet of abundance.

---

43 Stephen R. Covey, *The Seven Habits of Highly Effective People: Powerful Lessons in Personal Change* (London: Simon & Schuster, 2004), p. 157.
44 Covey, p. 317.

Knowing our values and living by them can stop us from becoming distracted by a sense of urgency. It can be difficult to remain loyal and focused on those values, so we need to be aware of the bigger picture. In this bigger picture we can be more mindful and better able to discern those things and activities that distract us from 'the one thing necessary'. These distractions are usually very subtle and are often things that are themselves of value; however, through our attachment to them, we turn them into false gods. We can become attached to our possessions, to our busyness or to anything that takes over the centre of our lives. Organisations, workplaces and religious institutions also need to acquire a mindful perspective – a meta-view, in order not to become caught up in the non-essentials, but to come back to the priorities. If we spend all our time stuck in the immediate and the urgent, we can become embroiled in a system that supports a culture of profits before people, results before values and sales before soul. Without a bigger picture or an awareness of what is truly necessary, we will remain directionless and uninspired. If we are all like Martha, distracted by so many things, there will be nobody prophetic in our world to inspire us. We need people who, from their stillness more than their busyness, steer us towards what is truly important. Getting caught up in the urgent and in instant gain, and seeing only that, drains our life of energy and inspiration. So, whether in our personal lives or in our working lives, we need to make space to step back, to look again at the direction our lives are taking. We need to become more mindful of the things that distract, clutter and drain our life of its real focus and energy. Both our inner and outer world is essentially shaped by what we give attention to.

View From the Hilltop

The sun was going down, the day beginning to close in. I watched from a distance, the cars and lorries looked so tiny as they passed on the busy road below. People were making their way home for the evening. Tomorrow they would again take their place in a busy line of traffic, seeking to get somewhere fast, to get through the hours; the same would happen the next day and the next. I had stepped out of it all for a little while and it felt both exhilarating and frightening. I had a glimpse of all that was transient, all the urgent things that would one day pass away. I saw the transience of my own life, my own preoccupations with things which I could not take with me to the banquet.

Jesus frequently went off to quiet places to view the bigger picture of his life and ministry. He also led the apostles up a mountain for reflection. Sometimes a mountain or hilltop can provide a powerful meta-view. It gives us a detached, clear perspective, from which profound lessons can arise. We get a momentary sense of what might be the one thing necessary and so become more attuned to the essentials and the non-essentials in our lives. It is in those times when there is a blurring of the boundary between time and eternity that we discern the essentials from the non-essentials. Hilltop views of our lives give us moments of temporary separation from earthbound consciousness; we glimpse how we are all part of one collective soul and that all that estranges us from that consciousness will one day pass away. This can be a transformative experience in awareness. People can sometimes encounter this in near-death experience, where the bigger picture and meaning of life comes more into focus. These instances actually become 'near-life experiences' in so far as they show us how to really live.

I knew that evening as I watched the world go by that even though I would soon be back again on those busy roads and in my busy life, something of this hilltop view would remain. Now and then, when I am in a hurry to get to somewhere or caught up in something that seems all-important, I pause and breathe and return again to that hilltop moment. In doing so, I notice all those things that will one day pass away. Life's little emergencies, seen from this perspective, become less urgent.

A Different Rhythm

A lot of the time we are anxious about being anxious and afraid of our fears. When we slow down our lives, slow down our breathing, we become attuned to a different rhythm, one not solely dictated by societal norms with all its strain and competition. While we may have many excuses for not taking the time to step out of these stressful conventions, much of our avoidance stems from our existential fears. We throw ourselves into activity instead of holding these fears about death and dying in an intentional mindfulness. When we neither deny nor immerse ourselves totally in them, we discover that most of these fears are really about losing the self we are attached to, our self-image. The Psalms advises that wisdom comes from keeping our mortality in mind: 'Teach us to count up the days that are ours, and we shall come to the heart of wisdom' (Ps 90:12). This 'heart of wisdom' lies beneath our anxious minds and shows us that most of our dreads are devoid of any real substance.

Striving or Arriving

It is often when life forces us to slow down that we learn how to live more fully. We notice our impatience: while waiting in a queue we notice how we fidget, looking at our watches, rechecking our list or texting – sometimes doing both at the same time. We habitually try to fill every spare minute: when we approach a pedestrian crossing, if the red light does not change to green straightaway, we press the button a second or even third time. We eat dinner whilst finishing off work, at the same time catching snippets of headlines from the news on the television. There is nothing wrong with multi-tasking, but many of our activities could become much less stressful and more meaningful if approached with a spirit of mindfulness.

If we live fully in the present moment, we can be mindfully aware of every step, every breath and every moment. When we return to the moment, we free ourselves from the many 'senseless' stories in our heads, which focus on a future that might never happen and a past we cannot change. We then view the present moment not just as a stepping stone to get where we want to go next but as inherently sacred in itself, a sacramental moment. In this way we can remain fully involved in our lives, while retaining a certain detachment at the same time. This results in a great easing off of stress, and so we are less likely to slide into the quicksand of anxiety. This detachment is not a superior kind of looking down on the world, but is more a spirit of non-resistance, a non-obsessing about the myriad thoughts, emotions and reactions that fill our minds every day. It is as if a part of us is peacefully watching the mental circus with all its tricks and gymnastics – we might even come to enjoy it. We discover that just as the seasons change, our bodies change, and everything in our life changes, with the exception of a changeless core within. When we begin to discover this core, we can, in times of difficulty, affirm that 'this too shall pass', and so there is less striving and more arriving.

The Fruits of Our Stillness

It is said that a field that is allowed to go fallow yields a richer crop the following year. Likewise for us, allowing fallow spaces each day can bear fruit. Stillness is not an escape from life; in fact it is often those who love to be busy and engaged with others who are called to be hermits, while those who love to be alone are called into an active life. As Dietrich Bonhoeffer said, 'Whoever cannot be alone should beware of community. Whoever cannot stand being in community should beware of being alone.'[45] This is a very good way to gauge if we are using mindfulness or contemplation to escape the challenges of everyday interactions and the complexities of community. How, therefore, do we notice the healthy fruits of silence and contemplation?

More than anything else, there must be evidence that our silence is facilitating the ability to listen more deeply. In moving from habitual to conscious mode, some people begin to notice a change in their tastes and preferences. They might seek out less aggressive music or films and more relaxed surroundings. Many people desire less sensory stimulation and more time close to nature. As a result of practicing mindfulness and reflection, one man has told me that he suffered from less disappointment, as he became aware that it was his own unreal expectations rather than other people that actually let him down. Some notice there is less yearning to be somewhere else, or to be someone else, and therefore they are less affected by advertising. There are fewer autopilot reactions; we begin to do things out of choice and from adherence to values rather than the need for

---

45 Dietrich Bonhoeffer, 'Life Together', *Dietrich Bonhoeffer Works*, vol. 5, G. Kelly, ed., D. Bloesch and J. Burtness, trans. (Minneapolis: Fortress Press, 1996), p. 83.

an adrenaline rush. There are fewer extreme highs and lows and less dependence on stimuli, especially those that lead to the inevitable slump of inertia afterwards. One woman told me she realised she had spent most of her life living in the past, hauling up old regrets, until finally she came to understand that while she cannot alter the past, she can stop repeating it in the present. Through the art of stillness we begin to assume more choice about our internal responses; there is less hurrying, even on those days where there are lots of things to do.

There are Things to Do

The sound of a single blackbird intruded my overcrowded morning and overcrowded mind. He asked me not to take this business of living so seriously. 'But,' I said, 'I have things to do.' The blackbird continued to sing, as if to say, 'I have things to do too.' Later that day there came a moment when the clouds in my mind momentarily parted and I remembered the blackbird; his sweet song was etched in my heart, while my mind insisted 'there are things to do'.

I looked around; a single rose, through her uncurled petals facing towards the sun, seemed to be saying, 'There are things to do'. In simply sharing who she was, this rose fragranced the world. Could I too unfold, uncurl and face the sun? Could I, like the rose, in simply being, fragrance the world? 'She's a bit too open,' my worried mind offered. I looked around; the sun twinkled as if to say, 'Listen to her.' I moved a little closer, her fragrance filled me and I felt there was a rose opening in my heart. I saw people passing by, weighed down with the heavy baggage of their own lives, their brows furrowed and shoulders hunched, laden with 'things to do'. They didn't stop to smell the rose, but she spread her fragrance anyway.

A nearby tree bowed down gracefully in agreement, branches tasseling in the wind. Yet its trunk remained anchored, its roots sinking deep into the earth. In its rootedness it offered shelter and shade; in simply being a tree it 'had things to do'. My hands unclenched, my toes uncurled, I stretched my own roots deep into the earth as my face turned towards the light. I dropped my shoulders and the heavy bags filled with my 'important life'.

Later, in the soft light of the evening the blackbird returned. I thanked him for showing me the miracle of attentiveness, for reminding me that we must stay awake, that we never know the day nor the hour when we will be asked to drop the baggage of our busy lives from our shoulders. I asked the blackbird to meet me again the next day and the day after, lest I forget how to live. I asked him to show me how to do what he does, to sing my song, especially on those days when 'there are things to do'.

A Moment for Mindfulness

1. Become aware of the present moment, the rise and fall of your breath. You might notice thoughts rushing through your mind; they may be telling you all the things you have to do. Neither deny them nor engage with them. Just return to the present moment, becoming rooted and anchored in the here and now.

2. Write in your journal about your life from a bigger-picture perspective. Write about what is truly important. What are you attached to? When does your list of 'things to do' prevent you from living with more mindfulness? What will you do more and less of in order to have more time to enjoy the bigger picture, the vista of the wonderful tapestry of life?

3. Rest with the words 'Be still and know that I am God.' In this stillness, notice the busy mind and what you tell yourself is really urgent or is the great emergency in your life. Can you create a little spaciousness around it and surrender it into the stillness?

4. A suggested closing blessing:

Today, may I, and all I meet,
slow down and savour life.
May we carry stillness within us
and stillness around us.

CHAPTER 14

A Seamless Flow:
Mindfulness in Everyday Life

The morning got off to a good start and people had settled into their retreats. I was facilitating the meditation for one group and a gentleman was taking another group next door. Two sisters arrived. One was attending my retreat; the other went in next door. At break time I popped into the washroom to wash my hands and overheard the sisters having a conversation between two toilet cubicles. One said, 'I am sick of that one now. I think I'll change over to yours.' The other replied, 'Yes, mine is very good.' I hoped I wasn't 'that one'. However, to my dismay, I heard, 'No, she's not great. I'm with her long enough, I think I'll change over to your fella.' Oh no, it was me she was sick of. Worse still, she had said she was with me long enough, and it was only mid-morning! I wondered if I should go now or listen more. I washed my hands a second time, scrubbing them in a mixture of fury and anxiety. I heard a few more mutterings but couldn't make them out as the voices were being drowned out by the sound of a toilet flushing.

My heart was like lead. The familiar volcanic eruption of self-criticism, with its usual torrent of disparagement and the 'not good enough' voice, was emerging. This was accompanied by a strange tightening in my chest and restriction in my breathing. Just as I was about to leave, I heard one of them say decisively, 'Yeah, I've made up my mind. I am going to change over to your doctor.' The contraction around my chest loosened and the world felt benign again. I was saved from the dreaded 'not good enough' dilemma for another while, and from the ruminating mind.

Unchanging and Eternal

'The world as hostile', 'the world as benign' are like pendulum states, dependant on the outer stimulus we are reacting to. The body responds to danger with the fight-or-flight response but it cannot distinguish between real dangers and those created by the catastrophising of the mind. The impact is the same: blood pressure is raised, the heart beats faster and hormonal and molecular changes take place. This internal pressure drains the nervous, adrenal and immune systems. We must note that it is our own reactivity to the stressor that causes the problem and not the stressor itself. It was *my reaction* to the women in the toilets that caused me to panic. Mindfulness, in teaching us to return to present-moment attentiveness, punctures this escalating reactivity. We discover a steady trust in something unchanging and eternal within, rather than allowing someone or something else to determine our centre of gravity.

Through the regular practice of reflective awareness we can become less entangled in what others think of us; because while we cannot live outside of relationship, if we see ourselves only through another's evaluation of us we will never be free. Furthermore, if we integrate our mindfulness with a spiritual dimension, we can ease into an awareness that we are cared for. We are then able to take ourselves a little less seriously as we gradually let go self-preoccupation, allowing our anxious selves to grow smaller and the divine life to grow bigger within us. We become more free of those automatic reactions, self-criticisms and habits that dull our ability to fully experience the present moment. We discover that as much as we might enjoy the good opinion of others, its impact is transient. In Thessalonians we are asked to pray without ceasing (cf. 1 Th 5:17). There needs to be a seamless flow between the stillness and balance we experience in designated times for meditation and the rest of the day and throughout all our interactions. So, while some argue that contemplatives should 'do something' more practical for the world, it is also true that by simply 'being' and by sitting in silent communication with the Spirit, the world is being transformed – the world within yourself and the world around you.

We often operate from one small compartment in the mind, dividing and labelling each experience as good or bad, pleasant or unpleasant, attaching ourselves to the former and resisting the latter. This can set up an inner battlefield where we tend to react habitually through avoidant patterns; this creates resistance and, of course, all resistance brings suffering. Clinging to what is pleasant is as problematic as clinging to pain. When we reside in only one familiar part of the mind, we miss the fullness of our experiences in the present moment. We easily drift into autopilot, running commentaries and sometimes catastrophic stories which the mind is adept at creating. A practice of daily attentiveness fosters a more philosophical way of looking at life and our experiences, not in an esoteric way but in a deeply incarnational moment-to-moment presence. This brings a new vitality to the most ordinary experiences. We can develop a way of being, whereby we are less consumed with passing things, no longer making 'our kingdom of this world', but becoming fully present to each event and circumstance, experiencing it fully and wholeheartedly, yet in a spirit of non-possessiveness. No matter what crisis or drama may exist, we can retain a certain connection with the ground of our being; an inner place of calm; a bit like Jesus in the boat, where he remained at peace even while the storm rose up around him. This is a disposition that can be cultivated each day, even amidst the changing winds of outside events.

Don't Forget to Smile

At the centre where I work, we frequently run silent retreats. One day a man came to check the elevator and curiously asked what all the people walking up and down the garden in silence were doing. I tried to explain that they were doing mindfulness meditation. He looked at me blankly, so I further explained how they were on a silent retreat, but got the same blank stare again. Eventually, I tried putting it in a different way: 'They are here for some quiet time ... to help find themselves.' He looked even more confused and, resuming his work, muttered to himself, 'Well they obviously don't like what they're finding.'

When we are silent we often look like we don't like what we are finding. This is usually because our minds have wandered off somewhere else. We leave the present moment through employing one or more of the following:

Denial: Ignoring or refusing to acknowledge the truth of a situation just as it is.

Repression: Burying the awareness and the associated feelings around an event or experience.

Projection: Directing our energy outwards onto some person or event; putting the responsibility for what is happening elsewhere.

Regression: Escaping back to the past, usually to some infantile state.

A practice of mindfulness reminds us to come back from the places we escape to, while spirituality helps us heal the hurts that made us run away in the first place. As children, we may have learned to 'check out' from places of unpleasantness or unmanageability, to go off somewhere else, to a world of fantasy, to a distant future where there would be no pain. We then ceased to 'be there', inhabiting instead a more elevated or perceived safe place. This strategy worked in many respects, but eventually adult life asks us to come back, to come home, to seek safety by embracing a oneness with what is here right now.

Making Friends with Ourselves

We tend to cling to the more pleasant parts of our personalities. For example, we may like to think we are always kind, compassionate and spiritual. Over-identification with the more preferred aspects of our personality causes splits in our psyche, because if we insist that we are always kind and so on, we will get a shock when we meet the not-so-nice parts of ourselves. If we say somebody is a shy person, we will put them into a 'shy' box; likewise, we might describe a person as an extrovert, whereas in truth no one can be reduced to any one characteristic. We need to make friends with the fullness of who we are, not with who we want to be. There is goodness in the worst of us and badness in the best of us, so it is best to embrace the whole lot. When we accept our experiences and personality traits with non-resistance, when we humbly embrace all of who we are, the wheat and the darnel, a peace settles in our heart. And that peace is not for ourselves alone – it impacts on everyone and everything around us, we bring a little *nirvana* to *saṃsāra*, a little bit of heaven to earth.

God of the Hair and Hair After

To become mindful of little things can bring a beautiful texture to our lives and to the lives of those around us. In a hair and beauty salon I have frequented over the years, there are sayings and verses on kindness and mindfulness dotted around. There is often a short reflection for you to read while you are waiting to be attended to at reception, a quotation on stillness pinned to the mirror, and the staff always greet you with sincerity, enquiring about your family or your health or things like that. There are little touches like pretty tissues for you to take or a little bowl of sweets for you to pick from, and there is always some relaxing music playing in the background. All of these touches are very subtle. 'Good for business' somebody remarked when I mentioned them, but I wasn't sure this was just about business. One day I asked the owner of the salon about it and she explained that her faith was important to her; that each morning she prays that her work will help somebody that day and she remembers to remain mindful and pray for them after they have left. She said she surrenders her day and her work to God. She went on to tell me how and why her spirituality had become meaningful to her: she was a humble, gentle woman who had known suffering. Since then, any time I go there, instead of talking about the weather or how exactly I want my hair to look, we tend to talk about other things: matters of the heart, life's challenges and so on.

Little things, little touches, can bring awareness and conversations of the divine into places we least expect. When ordinary days are approached as sacred, reception areas can become confessionals, hair salons can become cathedrals, and there can be touches of God in 'the hair and the hair after'.

Normal Day

Often we have to nearly lose someone or something before we see its true value. I had a health scare a number of years ago. I was very nervous in the week coming up to the appointment when I would be told if the results were benign or more serious. During this period I was acutely aware of all the things in life I take for granted and silently promised I would take nothing for granted after this. I emerged from the hospital, elated, so grateful that I had been given the all-clear. It was nearly five o'clock, so I got stuck in the homecoming traffic. I looked at the frustrated irritated faces of the other drivers – there were honking horns and bad moods everywhere. As I looked at the lines of cars, I thought of the lines of patients waiting for treatment in the hospital, some emerging with bad news. Some would do anything to have their problem today be just about a line of traffic.

I too had often been one of those irritated drivers, but today I was smiling in gratitude. Every delay at a red light was an opportunity to breathe and look around; I wanted to tell everyone that this ordinary day with traffic congestion was a blessing, that we would want it back if we were diagnosed with terminal illness. I decided I better start by telling it to myself – not to forget this epiphany. I remembered a poignant verse I had received many years earlier; one that did not mean much at the time but now resonated very deeply with me on this Friday afternoon:

Normal day, let me be aware of the treasure you are. Let me learn from you, love you, bless you before you depart. Let me not pass you by in quest of some rare and perfect tomorrow. Let me hold you while I may, for it may not always be so. One day I shall dig my nails into the earth, or bury my face into the pillow, or stretch myself taut, or raise my hands to the sky and want more than the entire world your return.[46]

A Moment for Mindfulness

1. Become aware of your breathing. Notice the many ideas and thoughts passing through your mind: planning tomorrow, comparing yourself to others, wondering why someone said something. Just notice the interplay of these thoughts. Do not add judgement, simply return to the present moment.

2. In your journal, write down all those characteristics you do not like in others. Next write 'I bring acceptance to …' before each of these traits. Can you make space for them? Can you broaden how you define yourself?

What do you dislike about normal days? Could it be that hidden in their ordinariness there lies an exquisite beauty? Maybe write a verse of praise for all that you are grateful for about normal days.

---

46 Mary Kay Mueller, *Taking Care of Me: The Habits of Happiness* (Forres, Inverness: Findhorn Press, 1996), p. 110.

3. Acknowledge and surrender those attachments to how you wish to be perceived (sensitive, wise, intelligent, funny, etc.). These are parts but not all of who you are. Ask that you may see the whole, the beauty of your own being, in every unfolding circumstance and in every person you meet today.

4. A suggested closing blessing:

May one bit of the world be transformed today;
the one within me.

CHAPTER 15

From Fear to Faith:
The Soul's Way

The storm rose and the rain got heavier as the car swerved from side to side; I was now battling a head wind. I turned up the volume on the radio, which reported that a strong storm was rising in the southwest. I gripped the steering wheel of my silver Toyota Starlet, my first car. The traffic, which had been heavy a few hours ago, seemed to have thinned out; it felt like it was just me and the rising storm on this open country road. It was at least another twelve miles to home; now it was dusk and the rain was turning to hailstones. The dusty sacred heart dangling from the front mirror suddenly caught my eye. I asked him to bring me home safely, but to my annoyance he remained expressionless, even sleepy; the dust making it seem as if his eyes were glazed over. So I called a bit louder, 'Lord save me!' I remembered the story of the disciples on the boat, also afraid of a storm, trying to wake up a sleepy Jesus. Like them I cried, 'Lord, do you not care?' Eventually I started bargaining and haggling: 'Lord, if you get me home alive I promise I'll enter a convent for the rest of my life.' Smugly, I thought to myself, 'That should do it, that should wipe the dust from his eyes!' After all, how could anyone, God included, refuse so great a sacrifice? Eventually the storm abated and I did get home alive. I took down the dusty picture and tucked it away where there were no more reminders of a sleepy Jesus or a beckoning convent.

Bargaining is often part of our way of getting something: if I give this, will you give that? If I make this sacrifice, will you grant me my request? The woman of Samaria started to barter when Jesus offered her living water; she said, 'Give me some of that water so that I may never be thirsty or come here again to draw water' (Jn 4:15). Hers was a domestic request, not coming from any particular interest in the spiritual journey. Yet this bargaining, while carrying mixed motives, can be an entry point to the spiritual journey. We may start out with the question 'What's in this for me?', but we may arrive at a very different question, one which asks, 'What is the greater purpose of my life?' The former is an ego concern; the latter is a spiritual one.

Sometimes people start out on a spiritual journey by learning relaxation techniques or by taking a mindfulness course. Their motive at that stage – perhaps to lower stress or become healthier – isn't spiritual *per se*. Eventually, however, deeper questions emerge and they no longer ask 'What's in this for me?', instead the voice of the soul rises and seeks to know 'How can I live fully, this one short and valuable life?' When you ask a new set of questions, you tend to receive a new set of answers. Yet, because we are human we tend to haggle and bargain, we hedge our bets. Many of our popular novenas have a bit of that bargaining: '*If I do* nine days, on the ninth day will my request will be granted?' This 'if I do' seems to surface before we make a commitment. Even Peter, when walking, and balking, on the water, said to Jesus, 'Lord *if* it is you …' We say something similar, we hold onto our ifs and buts and our what's in it for mes. As Daniel Ladinsky writes, it is as if 'God is trying to sell us something, but we don't want to buy just yet. This is what suffering is; your fantastic haggling, your manic screaming over the price.'[47]

That Sinking Feeling

We often look for a visible sign or an immediate answer when we are afraid. When the disciples were terrified of the storm at sea, they were irritated that Jesus was sleepy, so they woke him up to get an effective response. But Jesus modelled the deepest trust, asleep in a boat while a storm rose up around him. That kind of stillness can only come from a deep foundational faith, a belief that despite the power of the storm, we can be held up by something even more powerful: the waters of life, of trust, of protection. Often, the storms of our life will not be quietened immediately, but we may find a new stillness or strength within those very storms. Similarly, our prayers may not always result in the difficult circumstances being taken away from us, but a deeper faith can grow inside of us because of that circumstance. Authentic faith asks that we stop clutching to the sides of our boats. Real faith asks that we risk, take a step in faith and trust the water. It is when we focus on the obstacles and the fear, like Peter, that we begin to get that sinking feeling. The mystery of God is often described as being like the open vastness of the sea, we are invited out of our man-made little boats onto that sea; invited to take the hand being held out to us. When we trust and let go, we eventually become the hand for others in their own letting go.

---

47 Daniel Ladinsky, *I Heard God Laughing: Renderings of Hafiz* (Walnut Creek, CA: Sufism Reoriented, 1996), p. 13.

Stop What You Are Doing

Recognising when to let go is difficult. Kerry poet and philosopher John Moriarty put it most beautifully:

> Clear days bring the mountains to my doorstep, calm nights give the rivers their say; the wind puts its hand on my shoulders some evenings, I stop what I am doing and I go the soul's way.[48]

There are many times we are invited to stop what we are doing and go the 'soul's way'. The call to surrender doesn't always respect our plans; it doesn't always give us enough time to check our emotional thermometer to know whether we feel like letting go or whether we feel we are ready to go the soul's way. Scripture informs us that we never know 'either the day or the hour' (Mt 25:13). I used to find this a rather scary concept, often afraid to go to sleep at night in case 'the hour' might creep up on me. Now I like to think of it as meaning that we never know the day or hour when the wind puts its hand on our shoulder and we can surrender and embrace life rather than struggle against it. This is essentially what mindfulness is about: non-resistance. The ego, however, continues to create resistance; it tells us to hold on to our own control and tries to drown out the whisper of the spirit which is telling us to 'let go, trust the hand that holds you'. These whispers come not once in a lifetime, but every day.

Perhaps the annunciation is not just a historical occasion; maybe you too have had annunciations – those moments when you had to stop what you were doing (whether that was an addiction to some habit or substance) and instead

---

48 John Moriarty, *Nostos: An Autobiography* (Dublin: Lilliput Press, 2001), p. 491.

go the soul's way. When we respond to these invitations to surrender, we experience an opening. A softening of the heart and a sense of possibility replaces fear and rigidity. This is a much deeper experience than rattling off a few prayers in order to bargain or appease. This surrender takes the emphasis off of ourselves altogether, off of what we do. Instead we yield to that same spirit that visited Mary in the gospel – we allow something be done unto us. Faith, then, is not about the things we do or bargain for, it is something breathed unto us and through us.

The Soul's Way

Instead of bemoaning why so many say 'I'm spiritual but not religious', we need to stop what we are doing and listen again for how we can rekindle something of the soul's way. What many are trying to delete is often a God of judgement, one who critiques and criticises – a mere projection of our own internal critic. Who wouldn't want to delete that? The God of life, on the other hand, touches, invites and transforms through our life experiences.

Karl Rahner recognised that the Christian of the future will not be convinced by religious indoctrination without personal experience and advised we 'do something more than merely to take up a given rational attitude to the speculative problems of the divine, and to respond in merely doctrinal terms to the teaching of Christianity. We do need to work out a certain theology of mysticism.'[49] I have worked in ministry groups and retreat teams where we shared many 'doctrinal terms', while never alluding to or seeking guidance from the Spirit. We never, in any real way, shared our own everyday

49 Karl Rahner, *Christian Living Formerly and Today, Theological Investigations* 7 (London: Darton, Longman & Todd, 1966), p. 14.

faith. Perhaps too embarrassed, we hid behind ministerial language and religious and political debates. When we neglect the Spirit in our conversations to the extent that it is barely recognisable as the foundation to our work, we become spiritually dehydrated. We then become part of the what people find uninspiring. We lose our flavour, our salt; as the scripture warns us, we become 'thrown out to be trampled under people's feet' (Mt 5:13). Bishop Ignatius of Latakia, in an address given at the assembly of the World Council of Churches in 1968, said: 'Without the Holy Spirit, God is far away, Christ stays in the past, the gospel is a dead letter, and the Church is simply an organisation.'[50] Sadly, the life-giving gospel has often remained a 'dead letter', trampled on by hierarchical disputes and over-emphasis on structural changes rather than transformative renewal. This can seem lifeless to those thirsting for spirituality; those who desire a real encounter of the Divine in their everyday.

The inner impulse is first and foremost an initiative of the Spirit, an inner experience of the risen Christ, in which 'the cosmos is resurrected and groans with the birth-pangs of the kingdom, the risen Christ is there, the gospel is the power of life'.[51] Clinging to outside structures without this 'power of life', we become just a bundle of dry bones. While on earth, Jesus was a disturber of those who over-attached themselves to the outside structure, calling them instead to follow the Spirit: 'God is spirit, and those who worship, must worship in spirit and truth' (Jn 4:24).

When we define faith as merely a set of beliefs and doctrines that we must prove to be either right or wrong, instead of a

---

50 www.orthodoxresearchinstitute.org/articles/dogmatics/harper_holy_
spirit.htm (accessed 24 January 2014).
51 Ibid.

dynamic energy penetrating every area of our lives, we lose sight of the soul's way. Likewise, we can become so caught up with hierarchy that we become like the disciples when they were rebuked for their self-promoting disputes about which of them was the greatest (cf. Lk 9:46).

In the book of Isaiah, we meet an exiled group of Israelites; dispirited, tired, fragmented, they were not told to create more structures or documents or positions, but to be attentive, mindful, to 'listen': 'Listen carefully to me … Incline your ear, and come to me' (Is 55:2-3).

Rekindling the Spirit

We began in bright certainty,
your will was a master plan
Lying open before us.

Sunlight blessed us,
Fields of birds sang for us,
Rainfall was your kindness tangible.

But our dream was flawed;
And we hold it now,
Not in ecstasy but in dogged loyalty,

Waving our tattered flags after the war,
Helping the wounded across the desert.[52]

How do we reclaim that bright certainty, that master plan? Will we settle for 'dogged loyalty' instead of the ecstasy?

52 Pádraig J. Daly, 'The Last Dreamers', *The Voice of the Hare* (Dublin: Dedalus Press, 1997), p. 15.

Jesus, when on earth, emptied himself. He was so empty, mindful, detached from position, title or any self-reference that the invisible Spirit became luminously visible through him. The Spirit is always doing something new, recreating the old; if we are looking only in set places, we will fail to notice the many manifestations of the Divine becoming visible right here, right now. Maybe the mystics of the future that Rahner speaks of are in places we least expect; maybe they are uprooting the comfortable and pulling down princes from thrones.

Angels with Studs

I was trying to get onto a packed train from Rome to Florence. It was roasting hot and I was on crutches at the time. Just as I managed to get on, I noticed there didn't seem to be an empty seat. In fact there were lots of people standing, squashed together. There was a tense, even angry, atmosphere on the carriages, everyone fighting for their corner. There was also an overpowering smell of perspiration. So as well as being afraid of getting trampled on, I felt nauseated. I was annoyed as I had been told my ticket had a seat number on it, but now I could hardly see a seat, let alone a number. I couldn't move forwards or backwards, until eventually I spotted a tiny, silver-haired, ruddy-skinned woman sitting on the ground, an unlit cigarette hanging from the side of her mouth. She got up, came over and said something to me in a rather gruff voice, but I couldn't understand her strange accent. She narrowed her blue eyes, piercing me like arrows, and repeated it in a shrill voice. I tried to follow what she was saying but all I saw were her stained, gappy teeth holding onto the end of the dangling cigarette. I was still struggling to make out what she was saying when she grabbed the ticket from my hand. She shuffled through the crowds, barely visible, waving my ticket in the air. Perspiration flowing down her face, she took a shabby handkerchief from inside her t-shirt and wiped her forehead, looking as though she was bracing herself for a momentous task. She was; she stopped in front of a large, angry looking man who was slouched half asleep. She said something loudly to him, pointed to my ticket and pointed to the seat he was sitting in. The man did not move so she repeated what she had said and repeated her gesture. He still did not move so the woman kicked him lightly in the shin. He looked up angrily, but still he did not move. The woman kicked him again, a little more forcefully this time. The man stood up and growled down at her, probably hoping his size would intimidate her, but the woman straightened up to her full four-foot-nothing stature and, hands firmly on hips, once more showed him the ticket. The large man looked at it, sneered at the woman, then made a rude hand gesture. She quickly returned the same gesture! She pushed him again, and though she only reached his knees he staggered and began to look a bit wary of her. Eventually, he dragged his bag off the seat and shuffled away, muttering to himself. I kept my head lowered as she beckoned to me to take my seat. I thanked her and she said nothing. I was about to ask for her name but she was suddenly gone, making her way again through the tightly packed bodies to uproot some other unsuspecting lodger.

The Spirit All Around Us

I always thought of angels as ethereal and feathery. However I pictured them, I didn't imagine them perspiring or that they might make uncouth hand gestures. I always imagined they would tap us lightly on the shoulder if they wanted to tell us something – not kick us in the shin! Normally I look up to the sky if I want to imagine an angel. I certainly don't expect to look down and see them smoking a cigarette on the ground. Maybe some angels are like Jesus in the gospel: turning tables (or seats) upside down and pulling princes down from their thrones. Maybe they are uprooting the powerful and raising up the lame. Both the Old and New Testament mention angels: they appeared to Mary, to the shepherds, to Zechariah, as well as to Jesus in the desert and in Gethsemane. The word 'angel' comes from an old Greek word meaning 'messenger'. Maybe these messengers are all around us, maybe we do not need to go looking for them; maybe they are sitting at our tables, working at the checkout, sweeping the street, driving buses, reaching for our hand, touching our shoulders and, when necessary, kicking us in the shin. We need to be aware and awake, because at any moment we might see an angel – we might even see one when we look in the mirror.

When we introduce awareness of the Spirit into our everyday life, we will see revelations of the Divine where we least expect them. They are often the little ones but they call us to change, they disturb the status quo and bring fire to the world around them. Yet they rarely know they are angels, they just go about their day, going the soul's way.

A Moment for Mindfulness
1. Bring attention to the present moment. Notice the storms in the mind, the holding on, the control, the bargaining: 'If I do this, will you do that.' Simply notice, do not add another layer by judging or commenting. Bring awareness to your breathing; notice any softening or expansion, any glimmer of the opening to the Spirit.

2. Write the dialogue between the part of you that wants to 'leave what you are doing', and the part that is afraid. How is the Spirit inviting you to rekindle your wonder, to reclaim your flavour? When has the Spirit surprised you by sending angels when and where you least expected them?

3. Notice how the Spirit is attracting you to go the soul's way. Notice how the mind wants to hold on. Allow both the attraction and resistance to coexist; simply rest and lean into the embrace of God.

4. A suggested closing blessing:

> *May we each be the hand for one another;*
> *the one that helps another along the soul's way.*

CHAPTER 16

Tuesdays with Julia: Mindfulness and Memory

Today my thoughts turn to Julia, a close friend and soulmate for over twenty-five years. She died a year ago today. Julia and I met every Tuesday for breakfast; we shared many dreams and hopes together. She was one of those people who had the gift of reminding others of their best selves. She had a way of shining light into people's hearts and igniting their magic. I am one of the many fortunate people who received and was nourished by Julia's magical presence. With Julia, there was always something new to be excited about. We both loved exploring new concepts on matters of spirituality and awareness and would reflect on new insights we had extracted from the scriptures when we met each week. We always seemed to have some new dream to share, some new plan or goal. And those times when the plan went astray, Julia would offer her notoriously habitual assurance: 'Sure that's all right too.'

Whenever something difficult emerged in between our weekly meetings, I would find myself thinking, 'What would Julia say about this?' It was a comfort to know that whatever it was, we would share it on Tuesday; a comfort to know, not just that Tuesday would always be there, but that Julia would always be there. Her presence was one of life's few constants (she used to say repeatedly, 'Anytime, day or night, just remember I am always here'). Maybe that is why I employed so much denial during her short illness and unexpected death.

Like many others, my heart was breaking as Julia died. Not for Julia herself, because we all felt that she was on her way to the banquet she so believed in, it was breaking more for myself and all the others who shared cuppas and chats with Julia. What would Tuesdays hold now? Who would soften the hard edges of life by reminding us 'that's all right too'?

Sea of Nothingness

One day, while walking by the beach, I finally had to admit to myself that there would be no more Tuesdays with Julia. I felt cheated, like the disciples must have felt on the road to Emmaus. The roar of the sea was haunting me, the endless boundless sea which had no beginning and no end. I was despondent – my life seemed to be so full of endings. I looked blankly at the sea. Normally I would find it so energising, but today it seemed hostile, threatening, deadening. In fact everything around me seemed hostile and dead, which seemed to confirm that life is nothing more than a valley of grief. For what seemed like hours, I strolled aimlessly. In the end I couldn't remember the entrance I had come through on to the beach. I did not know the direction I had come from or where I was going. There was nobody else around, just myself and the sea, which increased my sense of abandonment. I looked out again onto that formless sea. 'Where is Julia now?' I asked nobody in particular. 'Where are they all now? Where is my mother? Where is my father? Where are those who walked with me, those whose lives and hearts I shared, where are they all? Is it all over or does something lie beyond?' A single wave crashed onto the beach, carrying off the tiny little shells and stones, sweeping them up mercilessly in its clutch and thrusting them into its foam. 'Does death just sweep us up until we are no more?' The violent crash of another wave seemed to roar even louder now, as if to say, 'Can you not see? Death just swallows you up. You will be like these helpless little pebbles and nothing will remain except this vast, haunting silence.' I shivered; I did not want to believe that, I did not want to believe that death just wiped us away. I wanted to know that my parents and Julia and all of them were there somewhere. I started to cry. 'Too many losses ... I don't know what I believe in anymore.' Does death really have the final word? Are we really like insignificant pebbles waiting to be thrown into the sea of nothingness? I felt a bit guilty at this unfamiliar non-belief, and guilty that I was angry with God, and maybe even a bit angry with Julia too for leaving.

Stronger than Death

I continued to walk aimlessly, sulking with God, sulking with Julia, kicking a pebble out into the sea and muttering 'It's not fair' until I imagined a response, one like Julia would give, in her own compassionate, mischievous way. In that moment it was as if she was walking with me, even giving me another pebble to kick, reassuring me that being angry was 'all right too'. Now I was both laughing and crying as I kicked more pebbles, remembering the many outdated beliefs and ideas we'd 'kicked' together and the many jokes and funny incidents we shared. Splashes from a wave seemed to break the cold numbness, the tears and the laughter began to melt my lifeless spirit and I became aware that while there would be no more Tuesdays with Julia, something beyond and bigger than the confines of

Tuesday would live on. Those ripples of laughter that I was remembering now could not die, the spirit of friendship could not die, the spirit that drew us together could not die, something was stronger than death: the part that lived on in my heart. My step became lighter, my heart softer. Yes, love was stronger than death, friendship was stronger than death; the laughter and trust could not die because it was still alive, just by my remembering – even more than remembering, it was somehow within me. I realised that Julia's lighthearted and compassionate presence was no longer coming from the past; neither was it confined to a Tuesday or any particular day in the week, or even belonging totally to Julia's personality, because it was of the spirit that, while dwelling within her, also dwelt beyond her. It was everywhere, beating in the very heartbeat of life, while also beating in tandem with my own heartbeat. It was bubbling up from a place that had no beginning and no end, no limitations of time or space; it was boundless, formless, timeless and limitless, like the sea in front of me.

'I Am With You Always'

People we have loved and who have passed on can leave something of their essence behind; the imprint of their spirit, their attitude, can live on in our hearts. Those who walked with us for any length of the journey can leave a fingerprint on our hearts. We can continue to be nourished by the unique gift that they offered; we can continue to be strengthened by our relationships with them. When we treasure all of this in our hearts we feel immensely rich because we encounter them, no longer on the outside, not limited to their particular character structure, but now as part of a greater infinity, becoming an interior source of inspiration and love. So, Julia was not giving a false promise when she said, 'I will always be here'. It dawned on me slowly: didn't Jesus say something similar? 'And look, I am with you always; yes to the end of time' (Mt 28:20). Did he not also have to die, leaving those he loved behind yet living on with them, and with us, through an indwelling spirit? So now on Tuesdays, though I still feel an empty ache, sometimes when I come to a fork in the road, I pause to think, 'What would Julia say about this?' and somehow I get a sense of the route to take − always a compassionate one. Or now and then, when I realise that I took the wrong road, I find myself saying, as Julia would, 'Sure that's all right too!'

Death is often seen as the thief of life, the end of the road, yet in some cultures it is seen as a rebirth. In India, death is celebrated as liberation, while Native Americans see death as a natural transition, a seamless unfolding from the physical to the non-physical. Some cultures bury their dead in the foetal position in the earth: a symbol of their belief that death is not the end but a rebirth.

It's Going to be Great

Recently I visited a woman who was near death. She was a good woman, but she was annoyed with a man in her parish: 'Maybe I will be able to sort him out from the other side,' she said. It seemed totally natural to her that the relationship could continue to evolve and heal (or whatever she meant by 'sorting him out') beyond death. She said she would say a few prayers for him, but first she paused, smiled and called him a few colourful names! As she approached death, she said she was having dreams of being a child again, recalling springtime on the farm where she grew up and her delight at newborn calves and lambs. She saw her parents there, everything was new; she even smelt the manure again! She turned to me excitedly and said, 'You know, I think it's going to be great!'

Some say that we die as we live, so maybe each day we can be mindful of our ongoing journey with those who have died. We can hold on to the possibility that they are still supporting us on our journey, until we meet them again where 'it's going to be great'.

Poetry from Heaven

When I remember my father, I remember an empty space, one that neither of us could cross. This empty space was like a death before a death, which seemed to loom continually as his illness deemed him absent even while he was present. A sickly silence stood between us. Each time I saw my father's sad, pale face behind his grey chequered cap, I felt it was my fault; I wasn't good enough, I had somehow disappointed him. The 'sickness' felt as if it was within me, rather than in him. I vowed to myself that I would try harder, so I often put on oversized wellingtons and headed off with a big stick to bring in the cows for milking, hoping he might be watching proudly through the window. At other times I would bring in blocks for the fire; heavy blocks that were difficult to carry but seemed worth the effort if they got me just one glance of acknowledgement from beneath the grey cap. These blocks did not feel half as heavy as the blocks in the heart of one who believes they are a disappointment.

When my father died, I died a little too. I told myself I did not really miss him – my head told my heart stories – and while I no longer continued to put on the oversized wellingtons, instead I tried on wrong-fitting roles and duties, unconsciously still looking back for his approving face at the window. What I was doing was outside my awareness, a kind of 'whistling past the graveyard'.

Sometime after his death, I found my father's faded grey cap. It smelled of the farm, it smelled of Dada, it seemed to be telling me that he was gone, that he would not be coming back to the window. Most of all, it told me that I missed him. That moment of returning to my senses, to smelling the cap, broke the cycle of stories in the head. As I cradled the cap, I noticed something that made me sad - it was torn in the inside. Holding that imperfect cap with the torn lining, I felt somehow close to my father; it was as if we were of the same fabric. Strangely, I felt more connected to him now than I had ever felt during his earthly life.

In some teachings of mindfulness meditation, the word *samatha* features, which means 'stopping'. I like to think that in our stopping to remember those who have died, everything is in the present, including the lives they have lived. Perhaps then not only is something in ourselves set free, there may even be a setting free for our ancestors and those gone before us: 'When you can take a step as a free person, all your ancestors present in every cell of your body are also walking in freedom.'[53] In the Christian tradition this is called the 'communion of saints'; we let go of ego attachments and bondages which can bind us from generation to generation, and we embrace the blessing they now wish to pass on to us, a blessing that sets us all free. Eventually, we begin to connect with a place beyond the pain, as did the poet Brendan Kennelly in 'I See You Dancing, Father':

---

53 Thich Nhat Hanh, p. 30.

I go back beyond the old man
Mind and body broken
To find the unbroken man.
It is the moment before the dance begins,

Your lips are enjoying themselves
Whistling an air.
Whatever happens or cannot happen
In the time I have to spare
I see you dancing, father.[54]

Dancing Backstage

I knew a man who had a wonderful singing voice, but very
little confidence. I asked him to be part of a stage production
which I had written and was directing. The part I gave to
him required him to sing solo. He was terrified, and at each
of the rehearsals he seemed to lose a note or falter. On the
opening night, in front of a large audience, he began to sing,
and suddenly the power of his voice and presentation filled
the theatre and left us all breathless. Later he explained, 'I
seemed to get this awareness that my parents were behind
me, and were applauding me backstage; it was as if they were
even dancing to the music, urging me to sing my song to
the world.' This was a healing experience for the man, as
the only living memories he had of his parents was of their
own fear: they never encouraged him to sing; in fact, they
tended to discount anything creative or new and their lives
were spent worrying about what the neighbours might
think – certainly he never saw them dancing. In taking a
deep breath and releasing himself from the grip of his fearful

54 Brendan Kennelly, from 'I See You Dancing, Father', *A Time for Voices:
Selected Poems 1960–1990* (Tarset, Northumberland: Bloodaxe, 1990).

ego, he had returned to his true self, his true home where 'we feel peaceful, safe and happy, the place where we can be in touch with our ancestors, our friends, our descendants'.[55] In touch with his ancestors, this man sensed they were now free from the ties that bound them to things of the earth; even free enough to say, 'Sing your song, sing your song to the world.'

A Moment for Mindfulness

1. Bring awareness to the moment. Notice the stories your mind tries to tell your heart. Allow your breathing to create a bit of distance from those stories so that you can listen more deeply to the heart. Notice any emerging feelings of loss or grief; just be with them, neither denying or adding commentary.

2. Take time to remember those whom you have loved and lost. Write in your journal about the legacy they left behind. How might you want to honour their place in your story? Write a few lines, a verse, maybe even a song, to celebrate who they were, who they are now, and who you are from having known them on your life's journey.

3. 'Come to me you who labour and are overburdened, and I will give you rest' (Mt 11:28). Visualise dropping the weight and burden of your ungrieved losses, so that you can carry the memories in a different way and in a different place in your life.

---

55 Thich Nhat Hanh, p. 32.

4. A suggested closing blessing:

May we all be one,
including those who have gone before us.
In this oneness, may we become free,
as we take our place in the great web of life.

CHAPTER 17

The Web of Life: Karma or Grace

Prompted by grey skies and January blues I went to the travel agent in search of winter sun. I asked if there might be anywhere I could be guaranteed sun in January? To my surprise, she said, 'Actually, yes, in Puerto Rico, Gran Canaria.' She went on to say how she had never heard anyone saying they had bad weather there, explaining that it is a particularly sheltered part of the island that seems to have a continuous sunny climate. What more could I ask for? I booked for Pat and myself to go for a week to a particularly nice hotel recommended by the travel agent. 'Might as well treat yourself,' she said, handing me an invoice that was sure to drain the last of my funds earmarked for paying back the Christmas credit card debt. Bags were packed and our moods lifted with thoughts of escaping to the sun. I pored over the beautiful glossy brochure – long beaches, blue skies and the stunning hotel, which the travel agent had informed me had no more spaces available following our booking. 'Ah, you must have good karma,' she said half-jokingly. Later I boasted to a friend who also said, 'Lucky you, good karma obviously.' I smugly told her I wouldn't be around for a week and sympathised with how she and and everyone else would be freezing cold while I would be soaking up the sun.

The morning for departure arrived. In the airport we chatted idly to a few more passengers boarding our plane. The gentleman behind me said, 'The weather forecast is very bad for Gran Canaria for the week – storms and heavy rain.' When I noticed he wasn't joking, I replied, 'Nonsense, we're going to Puerto Rico, the part that has guaranteed sun all year round.' He smiled, but the smile did not reach his eyes: 'Hopefully the forecast is wrong.' 'Negative thinking' I decided and dismissed what he had said and went back to reading 'Tips for a golden tan'.

Sure enough we arrived to beautiful sun and to a hotel high up on the rocks with a striking view of the ocean. We were on the top floor and the entrance to the room was from an outdoor balcony, so each time you needed to go downstairs you did so out in the open. There was also a glass lift, from which it seemed you could see halfway across the world. 'Good karma!' I said as I ignored the weather map displayed at reception. I woke the following morning to the sound of something like air blowing – maybe it was already so hot that the air conditioning had to be turned on. Then a sound of splashing at the window – maybe they were washing them to ensure we had a speckless view of the ocean. 'Ah, this is the life,' I thought as I snuggled down into the duvet, 'I'll wait till they have the windows washed and then I'll have a lazy breakfast on the beach.'

Alas, the air blowing was not air conditioning – it was a circular wind starting to rise. The splashing sound against the window was not somebody washing – it was hailstones. This could not be. Wasn't this the place for guaranteed sun? I got up, went to get the lift downstairs; there was a notice on it which read 'Out of order due to electrical storm'. In howling wind we walked from the very top floor on the outside balcony, rain and hail blowing into our faces. Eventually we arrived at reception to see the weather chart with 'severe weather warnings'. No boats were operating and there were warnings about falling trees. The torrential rain and thunder storms continued all day, and the next day, and the next. We were freezing cold. Restaurants brought in all the outside furniture; at the pool, deckchairs and sun loungers were folded up. We continually heard people say, 'It's going to be like this all week,' worse still, we heard someone say, 'but it's to be sunny again next week.' 'How unfair,' I muttered, 'it'll be sunny again just when we've gone.' I was going to scream if I heard one more person exclaim how the rain and storms were 'extraordinary for the time of year'.

After a horrendous plane journey affected by the storms, we eventually arrived back home. To make matters worse, we heard that there had been lovely weather in Ireland all week – 'extraordinary for the time of year'. 'Bad karma,' people said when we told them. To make matters worse, one man said, 'Gosh that's strange, we go to Puerto Rico every year and always get sun. We are always very blessed.' Sometime later I had reason to go back to the travel agent. I asked after the lady who had guaranteed the sun and I was told she had left … 'To Puerto Rico, I hope,' the 'less blessed' side of me muttered.

Punishment and Reward

'Good karma' and 'bad karma'. Sometimes, we throw around clichés about karma as if the central tenet is a punishment/reward system, whereas, in fact, 'reaping what we sow' is a subtle phenomenon. Some would say that it can span across generations; it certainly spreads through our everyday connections in much more complex ways than often superficially understood. We are all interdependent and connected in this reaping and sowing, in both positive and negative ways. When we do something good, we do not immediately get a reward. Likewise, people who do bad can seem to be living flourishing lives. In Hinduism, according to the Vedas, if one sows goodness, then that is what one reaps; if one sows evil, then one will reap evil consequences. Life is compared to a field, in which karma is the seed.

'What goes around comes around' is another popular interpretation of karma. It can, however, be unwise to cherry-pick phrases from a culture or philosophy and use them as a way to justify why bad things happen to good people. 'You get what you deserve' is a very superficial and judgemental way of explaining apparent good or bad fortune. The prophets of old continually wrestled with these questions. Jeremiah lamented, 'Why is it that the way of the wicked prospers? Why do all treacherous people thrive? (Jer 12:1). It is as if he wants to know if good karma follows good deeds, or if it is all random, or 'should evil be returned for good?' (Jer 18:20)

All Creation Groans
We are all aware that suffering is part of life. There seems to be an inherent groaning in all creation, a brokenness passed on from generation to generation, as well as a tendency in us to operate from the dysfunctionality of the false self. Thomas Merton describes this human condition as

> the sickness that is present in the inmost heart of man estranged from his God by guilt, suspicion and covert hatred. If that sickness is an illusion, then there is no need for the Cross, the sacraments and the Church.[56]

56 Thomas Merton, *Contemplative Prayer* (New York: Doubleday, 1996), p. 107.

Anne Wilson Schaef, in her book *When Society Becomes an Addict*, addresses this collective need for transformation. She describes society as a system in need of healing, which like any addiction requires surrender to a higher power:

> What happens is that the addictive system creates God in its own image to suit its own purposes. This is an integral part of the delusionary nature of the system. That distortion further separates us from our spirituality and our awareness of ourselves as spiritual beings.[57]

There is, and always was, an ongoing human search for healing and liberation from the 'delusionary nature of the system'.

When Mindfulness Becomes a God

Something as attractive as 'self care' can lead us to create a god in our own image to suit our own purpose. I have experienced (and perhaps even facilitated) self-awareness courses that fostered an individualism and personal development that bordered on idolatry. The constant insistence that you 'look after yourself' can become as much part of the 'delusionary system' as the imbalance that occurred when we were encouraged to 'think of our neighbour and forget ourselves'. There is a growing emphasis on leaving others to 'take care of their own stuff'. It is indeed important that we do not take on misplaced responsibility, and many of us need to find that balance, but to be overly focused on self-care can be a very limiting way of engaging with life. Our hearts are made

---

57 Anne Wilson Schaef, *When Society Becomes an Addict* (San Francisco: Harper & Row, 1987) p. 91.

for otherness, for expansion and for connecting empathically with *their stuff* as well as our own.

A woman was walking down the street when she witnessed a man fall badly and hit his head, which began to bleed profusely. She said, 'I got an awful fright until I suddenly remembered all that I had learnt in first aid, so I quickly did my breathing exercise, bent down and put my head between my legs to keep from fainting.' She explained that when she looked after herself she felt fine again. By focusing so much on herself, she missed the whole point of learning first aid. Likewise, self-awareness and self-care could lead us to estrange ourselves from the pain of humanity. Sometimes the self-contained cosmos we create, with its incessant 'working on ourselves' mantra, has to give way to allowing the spirit to work in us and through us, and lead us out into the world of others. While mindfulness and self-awareness are helpful remedies in correcting the imbalance of self-neglect, a healthy spirituality leads us to discover that to love ourselves and love our neighbour are not mutually exclusive, but flow creatively into one another.

Like the tall trees standing independently outside my window, entwined by their underground roots, we too are entwined with one another at root level: 'We are so intimately joined in Divine Mystery that when a single one of us falls, we are all wounded.'[58] We impact upon each other at a verbal, atmospheric and vibrational level, by what we give and by what we withhold as we go through life. The measure you give out will be the measure you get; 'the standard you use, will be the standard used for you' (Mt 7:1).

---

58 Gerald G. May, *Will and Spirit: A Contemplative Psychology* (San Francisco: HarperOne, 1987), p. 321.

A Rough Crowd

I sat for hours in the courtroom. It is strange how we tend to be sent to the very places we may have always said we could not go. Even hearing about people with convictions in the news disturbs me. No matter how grave the crime, I am acutely aware that what divides the convicted person and myself is a very thin line. I become aware of my own transgressions and how lucky I am that my sins are not splashed all over the newspaper or broadcast on television. I always silently hoped I would never be called to jury duty, but now here I was in one of those places which the gospel reminds us we can be sent to even when we would rather not go. I witnessed many cases that day, as each person came before the judge to receive their fine, their sentence or whatever the judge deemed appropriate; yet I was not listening to the details of the cases, but found myself looking at the eyes of the convicted — most of which were downcast, sometimes hardened or dull, occasionally scheming, all beaten by life and beaten by themselves. No matter what case, I could still see that they were somebody's mother, father, brother. In fact, for one moment I felt each person was *my* mother, father, brother; the dividing line was dissolving, we were all of the one substance, whether we liked it or not. They, like me, like all of us, probably once had some dream for their lives, a dream for something more than what they were now faced with. Some people watched on with the same excitement as one watching a football match, wondering what the final outcome would be; others looked as though they were watching a crime thriller. For me, however, it was an experience that brought me to the edge of both my own and the collected pain of humanity.

My thoughts were interrupted by a well-dressed man who, half throwing his eyes up to heaven, said, 'Rough crowd here today.' I nodded, but something in me felt uncomfortable. I did not want to add another ounce of judgement to those who already seemed to be judged so harshly by life. I didn't want to 'take care of myself' by gathering around me the more respectable ones and dismissing the 'rough crowd'. The idea of segregating who my neighbour was circled in my mind: was each person here today my neighbour? Were they each my mother, my father, my brother? I remembered the moments along my own journey when I had glimpsed what mercy looked like; moments of received compassion. These memories had lingered in the background of my life, no matter what mistakes I made. Because of that, I could not separate myself from the 'rough crowd', today or any other day.

Of One Substance
Saint Anthony of the Desert said:

> God is gathering us out of all regions till he can make resurrection of our own hearts from the very earth, and teach us that we are all of one substance, and members of one another; for the one who loves his neighbour loves God, and the one who loves God, loves his own soul.[59]

I began to wonder if we can become liberators for one another's prison; if we are all 'members of one another'. This in no way excuses crimes committed, but it subscribes to the

---

59 *The Letters of St Anthony the Great,* Derwas Chitty, trans. (Collegeville, MN: Cistercian Publications, 1978), letter 6.

belief that people can change their behaviour; to the notion that the behaviour is not the essential core of the person and that the 'sin' is also the sin of society in its quickness to segregate and refuse second chances. I wondered if my sending a kind of prayer or blessing could make a difference here in the courtroom. At first I thought it might be a silly idea – how could *my* blessing make any impact? Then it occurred to me how much of an impact the absence of affirmation had already had on these people's lives.

The practice of loving kindness, which is encouraged in the teachings of mindfulness, encourage us to send a blessing to people – all people, not just those close to us. It is a blessing easily said: 'May you be loved, may you be at peace, may you be blessed.' Perhaps we can even 'stand in' and say the words that have never been said to another; maybe we can offer a silent apology on behalf of those who did not or could not give it; maybe we can even bless one another. His holiness, the Dalai Lama writes: 'As long as space endures, as long as sentient beings remain, may I too live, to dispel the miseries of the world.'[60]

On my journey home that evening I continued to be mindful about our place in dispelling the miseries of the world. I continued to see each of their faces before me. I saw the woman with the hardened eyes being taken away in the prison van. It clearly was not the first time she had been down this road, and probably wouldn't be the last. I thought of her little girl, who had been helplessly watching on. I grieved for both of them and found myself saying, 'May you be consoled.' Whose burdens, alongside her own, was this woman carrying? Could she be also paying the debts

60 H. H. Dalai Lama and H. C. Cutler, *The Art of Happiness* (London: Hodder & Stoughton, 1998), p. 191.

belonging to someone else? What was compelling her to repeat this destructive cycle again and again? I saw the man dressed in leathers and remembered the bizarre story he had told to cover his tracks for stealing. I did not believe his story but I wanted to believe in him, so I silently offered an affirmation in place of the person who had perhaps failed to affirm him. 'May you be blessed.' I saw the face of the tired judge, who occasionally seemed a little sarcastic yet had compassionate eyes. I found myself saying, 'May you be guided.' As I thought of each of them, I was reminded of the scriptural account of the criminal who was assured paradise as he hung next to Jesus on the cross. He was like all of those in the courtroom, those heads hanging in shame that day, full of self-hatred, bitterness, hopelessness and self-destruction. Some of their crosses were, no doubt, fashioned from their own self-destruction, but many of them had been fashioned long ago through invisible threads that bound them to the burdens and transgressions of others. On one level, it all felt so hopeless; my close proximity to them suffocated the part of me that wanted to establish my 'being different' to them. Yet in my heart I knew something else. I knew there was *someone* else. There stood one who once sat with and listened to tax collectors and sinners; someone who was right in the middle of the 'rough crowd'.

A Moment for Mindfulness
1. Bring awareness to your breathing and to present-moment attentiveness. Notice the judging that goes on, the incessant questions: 'Why does this happen?' 'Why does this not happen?' Do not get caught up in answering the chattering mind. Come back to your breath.

2. What have you complained about as being bad karma? What do you notice about repeating patterns in your life? Begin to write in your journal, allowing the journey of your life to emerge in your memory. Allow it all – do not add punishment or reward in your assessment of yourself.

3. Bring the picture of your life to the greatest love of all – the love that took upon himself your karmic debt and, in dying, offered up his own life for it.

4. A suggested closing blessing:

May I carry a glimpse of the compassion of Christ
to each person I meet today.

CHAPTER 18

Raisins for Happiness: It's All About Soul

John was a self-confessed mammy's boy who never learned to cook. I happened to be chatting to him soon after the death of his mother. I felt a bit sorry for him, knowing he had to now fend for himself. I asked him if he was looking after himself, if he was eating well. He assured me that he was eating fine. I decided to push it a bit further by asking what, for example, he had eaten that day. Proudly, he explained how he had gone to the supermarket that morning and bought a bag of buns, 'those tasty little ones with the raisins'. He went on to tell me how he had eaten them throughout the day, how they were 'the grandest things for filling you up. Sure you wouldn't know you were hungry at all when you have enough of them.' I was shocked. How could someone eat buns all day and not know their need for real nourishment?

On deeper reflection I realised that sometimes we all do exactly the same with our spiritual hunger: we fill up our souls with so many 'fast' fixes that we hardly realise we're hungry at all. These fixes, such as possessions, success and fleeting pleasures, can, like John's raisin buns, taste great at the time and give us a burst of energy, but ultimately they leave us undernourished, tired and empty.

Having Your Cake and Eating It

We can try to win the whole world, in all its instant successes and gains, while diminishing our inner lives and our connection with the soul. As Teilhard de Chardin writes:

> All these treasures, all these stimuli, all these calls coming to us from the four corners of the world, cross our consciousness at every moment. What is their role within us? They will merge into the most intimate life of our soul, and either develop it or poison it.[61]

The deeper hunger, created in us by the eternal, will keep gnawing away inside because we are made for something that transcends the normal levels of what we call 'happiness'. We have to be discerning as to what might nourish our inner life and not just look to fast fixes to fill us up.

The soul is surely not just something we have to keep an eye on to make sure it gets to heaven, but is more a place of connection with God, a place often called our 'essence', our 'eternal self', our 'wise centre'. Our souls contain a longing to connect with our home ground, to realise our deeper essence. Yet the soul, it would seem, also contains a yearning to embody something of our own truth, as experienced in this world and in human form. It is not so much a metaphysical entity put into our bodies, but more about 'that living sensitivity flowing deep within, often felt as a fluid yet definite sense of being oneself, a sense of inwardness, poignancy, or depth'.[62] Julian of Norwich described the soul as a place in the middle of her heart; it appeared to her as a

---

61 Teilhard de Chardin, *Le Milieu Divin* (London: Collins, 1960), p. 59.
62 John Welwood, *Love and Awakening: Discovering the Sacred Path of Intimate Relationship* (New York: HarperCollins, 1996), p. 50.

glorious city. Rumi imaged it as a tree growing fruit, while at other times he described it as a honey balm. It is sometimes spoken of as an intermediary bridge, connecting Spirit and body, form and formlessness, personal and universal. However you image it, soul-work needs to be embodied and grounded in the ordinary.

Much of what we call 'happiness' is dependent on some condition: I am happy because my family are doing well, I am happy because I have a good job, I am happy because I have found my soulmate. But what happens when one or all of these circumstances is removed? Is our happiness removed also? Throughout any one day, our levels of happiness can change frequently. Often we say 'It's a miserable day' because it's raining and we carry the rain in our hearts and on our face, or 'It's a beautiful day' because it's sunny and that brightens us up. God forbid that it's cloudy in the morning, sunny in the afternoon and raining in the evening because our level of happiness will be like an elevator going up and down all day! Likewise, we find ourselves happy on Friday and miserable on Monday. This gauge for happiness is fragile and unreliable. Through it we define happiness according to circumstance or something that we hope *will* happen: I'll be happy when I retire, when I get a promotion, when I have paid off the mortgage. When we attach our happiness solely to these things, we pin it on an elusive future and postpone our capacity to be happy right now. Likewise, when we compare our circumstances to others and wish for something other than our own lives, and our own story, we rob ourselves of a precious gift. We can amass any amount of stimulants, or any amount of 'I'll be happy when ...' scenarios, but none of them assuage the inner longings of the soul.

From Blobs to Roses

I started a course on calligraphy and wanted to make a present of a house blessing for a friend who was moving into a new house. I put a whole Sunday afternoon aside and it was late into the night when I finally sighed a breath of relief: 'It's finished!' It had been a long and difficult project but now it looked perfect. I leaned back to admire its perfection, holding the calligraphy pen in my hand. I shrieked in disbelief – a blob of ink dropped from the pen on to the page. I pulled the pen away quickly, only to discover a second one had landed further down the page. I went to try to dab the first blob before it would dry, only to end up making it worse. As I looked at it more closely, I noticed that its smudged edges assumed a shape, not unlike the outline of a rose. Holding my breath, I did the same with the other blob. There appeared another rose. Excitedly, I drew a winding thin line from one rose to the other, which took on the appearance of a stem. Then I sketched a few tiny leaves onto this stem and added another stem up the other side of the page. Now I gazed with wonder and awe: in front of me were the most beautiful roses brambled around the words, conjuring images of a country cottage. Interestingly, the first blob had dropped onto the word 'blessing' and now I agreed that the 'mistake' truly was a blessing, even though the perfect calligraphy did not go according to plan. When my friend received it she said, 'It is beautiful. I especially love the roses around the blessing, just like the roses growing around the door of my new home.'

Blobs can be transformed, mistakes can blossom into blessings. The perfect image in our mind is not often how the picture of our lives will unfold. When we reflect more deeply, we see blessings emerging from the places we called 'failure'. Something as beautiful as a rose can come from the things we have called our greatest mistakes.

Rosebuds in the Soul

The one question that will never disappear in the spiritual search is, 'Why suffering?' We will never fully comprehend why 'blobs' land on our lives or why bad things happen to good people. It can help to look at those times of limitation, suffering or failure in our own lives and think about what may have emerged from them. We may not find neat, clear-cut answers but we may begin to penetrate a little deeper into the soul journey or the Paschal Mystery in our own lives. Sometimes we will notice how a setback brought to birth some tender rosebud from the soul. John of the Cross wrote his most beautiful poetry during his nine months in prison, including 'The Spiritual Canticle' and 'The Dark Night of the Soul'. Julian of Norwich and Hildegard of Bingen experienced severe poverty and illness, and in their suffering produced the most inspiring literature and soaring music. Ignatius of Loyola, while in recovery from an injury, discovered the spiritual dimension to his life. He was previously a soldier filled with selfish ambition until he was injured in battle, after which he had to spend a long time in recuperation. During this time, he started reading books on the lives of the saints and his lofty dreams were transformed into something more soulful and grounded. His ambitious idealism was channelled in a new direction that changed his life forever. There are many reasons, usually only seen in hindsight, why life offers us these times of restriction or setback, which at the time look more like blobs than roses.

A work colleague told me about a time when he worked on a school retreat. The teenagers were sharing some of the difficult and unanswered questions in their lives and one of the lads, in support of his friend, advised, 'Just remember it will all be okay in the end, and if it is not okay, then it is not the end.' I don't know where the teenager had heard this wisdom, and I doubt that he was quoting Julian of Norwich's 'all shall be well, and all shall be well and all mannereth of things shall be well', but whatever its origins, he offered a wise and sensitive bit of advice, both for his friend and for all of us in our own unanswered questions.

How Do We Know?

'Fake it till you make it' is a poplar phrase used for motivation and has a semblance of wisdom in it, but living with soul takes us far beyond any technique or faking. Wearing a smile that does not reach your eyes does not inspire anyone and certainly does not create any ease or relaxation in your own body. We need to instead find those dismembered parts of our 'soul self' lying under the weight of our tired persona, sometimes under our joyless pleasures. In doing so we can excavate our natural laugh, our natural peace. Moments of mindfulness show us those times when we are most alive, and in so doing offer us more choice in how we can increase that aliveness.

A Little of What You Fancy

Nourishing the soul is often as simple as making space for those things that increase our love of life and add richness to our day. For some, that involves listening to music, reading poetry or looking at art. For others, communing with nature brings them into 'soul time'. Nobody can prescribe what little windows of wonder you can open on a daily basis to rekindle that immaterial essence within you that is free of social conditioning.

'A bit of red lipstick works for me when I'm having a bad day,' a woman once told me. 'Try it,' she advised, 'it does the trick every time. A bit of red lipstick and anyone can face the world.' 'A pink ribbon in your hair,' my mother said, whenever I was reluctant to go somewhere or was in a low mood. The red lipstick and the pink ribbon, even worn at the same time, didn't quite work for me, but these suggestions did set in motion thoughts about what little pleasures can brighten a day. Sometimes, we can dismiss the little things as silly, when in fact they could change the atmosphere of an entire day and remind us of the simple things in life, bringing feelings of being abundantly surrounded. 'The smell of freshly cut grass,' Mary said; while for Sue a few minutes looking up at the night sky when there is a full moon brings her to soul moments. 'Red underwear,' one woman confessed to me, 'for those times when I need to feel invincible. Nobody else might know the secret to my stride, but I do.' A man in his eighties, eyes twinkling, tells me how he still loves to dance; and while he does not have a dancing partner, he dances every day in his room. 'Like this,' he says as he twirls around and bows to the silent applause of his own soul.

So whether it is red lipstick, pink ribbons or the night sky, pondering on life's precious little things can give an overflowing sense of being cared for. It can lighten your step and remind you to be kind to yourself. We often hear the expression 'nourishing the soul', but in truth it is our soul that nourishes us; all we have to do is create space. You can build little windows for soul moments in your life. This may never win the applause of the world, but it will win your own applause.

You can, through daily attentiveness, withdraw from the pressures of our fast-paced world and tell yourself some good news, that which keeps awake your sensitivity of soul. You must stay alive to the wonder of it all. In the timelessness of soul moments, wisdom, beauty and compassion float to the surface. And don't forget you do not have to sit waiting at the sidelines, hoping for life to ask you to dance – you can start dancing in your own room! When you begin to dance, you notice the whole world dances with you.

What a Wonderful World

A busker was playing 'What a Wonderful World' on his button accordion. It was out of tune a little but it was the perfect backdrop for watching the passers-by in the town square. A man hobbled by with his dog who seemed to be hobbling too; they were in perfect time with one another and I wasn't sure who was taking whom for a walk. A couple walked by eating ice creams. He seemed to be suffering some disability, his co-ordination a bit wobbly; she walked slowly, accommodating his pace. A teenage girl passed wearing heels so high they made her look like she was walking on stilts. She looked at herself in every window she passed, as if searching for a reflection of the perfect image of a catwalk model. She threw a coin to the man sitting on the street corner; he was old, pale and sickly looking and he had a rabbit on his lap – an old, tired-looking rabbit. I winced when I thought of what would happen if one of them lost the other. The whole web of life was there: the beauty, the pain and, at some level, an innocent sweetness. We were all like musicians playing together, interdependent of one another. Some invisible connecting thread of vulnerability seemed to lie at the heart of it all. My own heart seemed to expand at the sheer beauty, and while I know that pain, cruelty and indifference will often separate us from this interconnected web of life, *a whisper in the stillness* reminded me that it was still 'a wonderful world'.

A Moment for Mindfulness

1. Notice your breathing – the in-breath and the out-breath. Allow thoughts, images and sensations to come and go. Do not chase after or try to get rid of them, just return to your breath and the present moment and rest for a few minutes.

2. Write a letter to yourself in your journal. Include in it some affirmation and celebration of the journey you have travelled. Keep it with you and read it on those days when you feel too tired to dance or when you forget that there are roses.

3. The blobs and the roses, the lipstick and the raisins: give thanks for all of it.

4. A suggested closing blessing:

> *It will all be okay in the end.*
> *And if it is not okay, then it is not the end.*